C000081253

The Salcombe Lifeboat Disaster

27 October 1916

Roger Barrett

Published by Salcombe Lifeboats

Any views or opinions expressed in this publication are solely those of the author and do not necessarily represent those of Salcombe Lifeboats.

Published in the UK in 2015 by the Salcombe Branch of the Royal National Lifeboat Institution, Salcombe Lifeboat Station, Unity House, Union Street, Salcombe, Devon, TQ8 8BZ.

www.salcombelifeboat.co.uk

Printed by Kingfisher Print and Design, Totnes, Devon

CONTENTS

The Bar

Out-along the folks are watching
    Where the Bar gleams white;
Wild and stormy is the outlook
    In the dawning light.
See! the lifeboat takes the water!
    They can hear their cries;
Now the breaking Bar they're nearing,
    Where the danger lies.
'Will they cross it?' They are asking,
    'Ah! She's lost to view!'
On the crest again she's mounting,
    And, 'Hurrah! she's through!'
Swiftly with the gale she's flying,
    Answering the call,
Where the shipwrecked souls are stranded
    On the rocks of Prawle.
Weary are the hours of waiting,
    Wives and sweethearts, pale,
When, from out the storm she's looming,
    Head against the gale.
But, the Bar! The crew are asking,
    'Is it aye, or nay?'
'Aye, she'll do it!' cries the cox'n,
    'Now my lads, give way!'
Suddenly a mighty billow
    Lifts her end o'er end .
Father have them in Thy keeping,
    And their homes defend!
Sacrifice supreme they offered,
    Every soul save two,
Men who simply did their duty,
    Yet were heroes true.
Henceforth when the Bar is breaking
    Sheer from side to side,
Salcombe lads shall hear the story
    How they nobly died.

Poem by R I Partridge from 'Songs of
Salcombe & the West Country'
published by Folk Press, London (1930)

1 HEROES ALL!

On Friday, 27 October 1916, the small town of Salcombe, on the South Devon coast, suffered a terrible loss when the lifeboat *William and Emma* capsized at the harbour entrance on her return from a fruitless mission near Prawle Point. Thirteen of her fifteen-man crew were drowned.

The Great War had been raging for over two years when the disaster occurred and many of the town's menfolk were away from home serving in the armed forces or aboard merchant ships. In France, the Battle of the Somme was in its fourth month and nearly 100,000 British soldiers were dead or missing.

Counted against losses on this scale, the death of just thirteen men may have seemed almost insignificant. Yet, even amidst the distractions of war, the disaster stirred the sympathy of the nation, with people from all walks of life contributing generously to the relief fund for the widows and children left behind.

For Salcombe's close-knit community the loss was devastating. Many of the townsfolk had seen the lifeboat capsize as it attempted to re-cross the Bar and return to the safety of the harbour. For them, the sight of those brave men – husbands, brothers and sons, friends and neighbours – battling for their lives within sight of their homes, had been almost too much to bear.

A century later, the tragic loss of those thirteen men is still etched in the town's collective memory. When, from the safety of the shore, one of the modern lifeboats – the *Baltic Exchange III* or the Inshore Lifeboat *Joan Bate* – is seen crossing the Bar in stormy weather, memories are awakened of that fateful day and silent prayers said for the safety of the brave crew. Today's powerful motor lifeboats may be 'light years' away from the 'pulling and sailing' *William and Emma*, but the men and women who crew them are no different – ordinary people who do an extraordinary job risking their lives for the safety of others. This book is dedicated to the crews of the Salcombe lifeboats and to those who wait anxiously for their safe return.

The modern Salcombe lifeboats: the all-weather Tamar Class *Baltic Exchange III* and the Atlantic 75 class inshore lifeboat *Joan Bate* (Chris Tizzard)

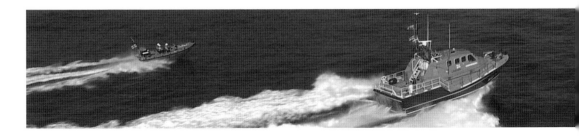

Contemporary postcard of the disaster by Alfred E Fairweather.
Of the fifteen men in the crew only W. Johnson and E. Distin survived.
(Fairweather Collection, Cookworthy Museum)

2 SALCOMBE & ITS LIFEBOATS 1869-1916

When the first lifeboat came to Salcombe in 1869, the small town, near the mouth of the Kingsbridge-Salcombe Estuary, was a thriving shipbuilding centre. Over two hundred wooden sailing ships, including the famous clipper-like Salcombe fruit schooners, had been built there since 1800. However, by 1890, shipbuilding and shipowning in the town had largely come to an end as a result of competition from iron and steam. Many of the town's mariners, and those engaged in maritime trades, migrated to larger ports such as Plymouth, Cardiff, Liverpool and Hull. Those that remained still sought to earn a living from the sea as fishermen, boatmen, pilots or coastguards, or by serving away from home in the Royal Navy or in the merchant fleet.

The coming of the railway to Kingsbridge in 1893 led to the growth of tourism in the area and, in the years leading up to the First World War, the unspoilt beauty of the harbour attracted increasing numbers of yachtsmen. Through all these changes Salcombe remained a tight-knit, almost insular, community where families inter-married and where everybody knew everybody else. It was this very inter-dependence that made the loss of thirteen men in 1916 such a tragedy, not only for their dependants, but for the whole community.

Returning to 1869, it was the wreck, near Prawle Point, of the clipper ship *Gossamer* of Liverpool in December of the previous year with the loss of thirteen lives (another unlucky thirteen), which prompted the RNLI to establish a lifeboat station at Salcombe. The first boat was a 33ft x 8ft 6in (10m x 2.6m), ten oared, self-righter named *Rescue*. The Earl of Devon presented the site for the boat-house at South Sands and the High Sheriff of Devon, Richard Durant Esq., provided the funds for both the lifeboat and the new building. The boathouse can still be seen today although it has not been used to house a lifeboat since 1925. During her time at Salcombe *Rescue* performed two services and saved two lives.

In 1887 the *Rescue* was replaced by the *Lesty* a 34ft x 8ft (10.4m x 2.4m), ten-oared self-righter. She was a foot longer than *Rescue* and fitted with water-ballast tanks to enhance her self-righting powers. Between 1887 and 1904 *Lesty* performed five effective services and saved ten lives.

When the time came to choose a replacement for the *Lesty*, James Distin, the coxswain, was looking for a boat with the handling ability and stability to get out across the Bar at the entrance to the

The lifeboat house
at South Sands
(RNLI)

harbour in the teeth of an onshore gale and back again safely through heavy seas. From his long experience as both coxswain and fisherman he knew just how hazardous the Bar could be. In January 1901, for example, it took all his skill to negotiate it when the *Lesty* returned from assisting the steamship *Pinedene* of Aberystwyth:

> At about 11.15 o'clock on Wednesday night, a message was received that signals of distress were being sent up about four miles off Prawle. Upon receipt of the news the lifeboatmen very promptly assembled and proceeded to launch the *Lesty*. There was a heavy ground swell, but the boat succeeded in clearing the Bar and was soon speeding in the direction of the signals ... At about a quarter past six [in the morning] the lifeboat returned to Salcombe and had a very exciting time on the Bar, which if inclined to break at all, is at its worst at low water. The Bar was very low yesterday morning. When, it was reached, a huge sea came roaring up behind the boat, raising the stern sufficiently to submerge her bow in the hollow of the wave to alarming depth. With rare skill the boat was kept end on, and in this position she was shot forward at a tremendous pace out of the broken water. (*Salcombe Times*)

Unlike her predecessors, the boat that James Distin and his crew chose to replace the *Lesty* in 1904, the *William and Emma,* was not a self-righter. At first sight, this may seem a surprising choice given the risk of capsize on the Bar. The circumstances that led to her

Salcombe Bar

Salcombe Bar at the entrance to Salcombe harbour, looking east to Limebury Point *(RNLI)*

Salcombe Bar is a ridge of sand at the entrance to the Kingsbridge-Salcombe Estuary. It extends south westerly from Limebury (or 'Lambury') Point on the eastern side. A heavy sea breaks over the Bar during southerly gales and, with the tide on the ebb, it is notoriously hazardous to cross. When the crew of the *William and Emma* made their forlorn attempt to re-cross the Bar at about 10.40am on 27 October 1916, it was 'blowing a hard SW gale with a high sea' and the tide was within two hours of low water.

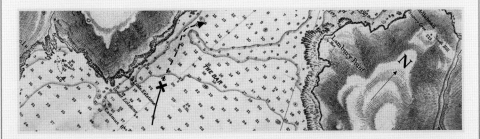

Extract from the 1927 Admiralty Chart showing soundings in feet. The *William and Emma* attempted to cross the Bar by the deeper channel on the western side but capsized at X. *(Admiralty)*

selection were set out in the Report of the Board of Trade Inquiry into her loss in 1916:

> In 1903, the lifeboat at Salcombe, which was on the self-righting principle, was getting old, and, an opportunity having arisen for her replacement, the Committee of Management decided to replace her. Accordingly, the then coxswain, James Distin (who was coxswain for twenty-six years up to the time of his retirement some six years ago), and two other members of the crew, Edward Quick and Edward Dare, inspected and tested lifeboats at Coverack and Looe. The Coverack boat was of the Liverpool type, and non self-righting, while the Looe boat was a self-righter. As the result of these investigations, application was made for a non self-righter of the Liverpool type, and in response to that request the *William and Emma* was supplied, and she was sent to her station at Salcombe on the 3rd of May, 1904.

The *William and Emma* at her builders, Thames Ironworks of Blackwall, London, before dispatch to Salcombe *(RNLI)*

At the first coroner's inquest, following the 1916 disaster, James Distin stated that 'the non self-righting boats were much more roomy and were better sailers'. Their 10ft (3m) beam, compared with 8ft (2.4m) in a self-righter, made them more stable and, according to the evidence he gave at the Board of Trade Inquiry, they were 'better sailers' because 'they went to windward better than the self-righters, owing to their end boxes being lower and holding less wind'. (The end boxes were air chambers fitted above deck at the bow and stern. In self-righters they projected above the gunwale).

Salcombe was by no means unique in selecting a non self-righter. At the end of 1915 the RNLI possessed thirty-four lifeboats of the Liverpool type, of which seventeen were about the same dimensions as the *William and Emma*.

The *William and Emma* was built in 1904 by the Thames Ironworks and Shipbuilding Company Limited, Blackwall, London, at a cost of £924, funded from the will of Mrs E E Cox of Weston-Super-Mare. The eponymous Emma Eliza Cox was the widow of William Masters Cox, a retired farmer who died in 1896. Emma died in 1901 at the age of 75, leaving an estate valued at £5543.

The builders, Thames Ironworks, had been established in 1837 and, by the end of the century, had become the largest shipbuilders on the Thames. The company was notable for producing iron work for Isambard Kingdom Brunel's Royal Albert Bridge over the Tamar in the 1850s and for *HMS Warrior*, Britain's first ironclad warship in 1860. It built over 200 lifeboats for the RNLI before going bankrupt in 1912. Today the company's most enduring legacy is West Ham United, 'The Hammers', which began life as the Thames Ironworks Football Club in 1895.

The *William and Emma* was 35ft x 10ft (10.7m x 3m) and weighed about 3¾ tons. When fully laden with crew, gear and water ballast, she weighed as much as 6¼ tons. For sail-power she had a jib and two lug-sails (mainsail and mizzen). She was also fitted to pull twelve oars having all six thwarts double-banked. With coxswain, second coxswain and bowman, she carried a crew of fifteen.

Before being sent away from London, the *William and Emma* had undergone extensive harbour trials under different conditions and had been thoroughly tested for stability. From the time of her arrival at Salcombe in May 1904 and the date of her loss, she was inspected on twenty-two occasions by the District Inspector of Lifeboats. During an inspection in November, 1907, she was exercised in a moderate SW gale, force 6 to 7, when there was a heavy sea on the Bar, and was reported to have 'behaved admirably both under sail and oars'.

Prior to her loss, the *William and Emma* had been launched for service five times but had made no rescues. Her first service was in

William & Emma
35ft Liverpool Class Lifeboat

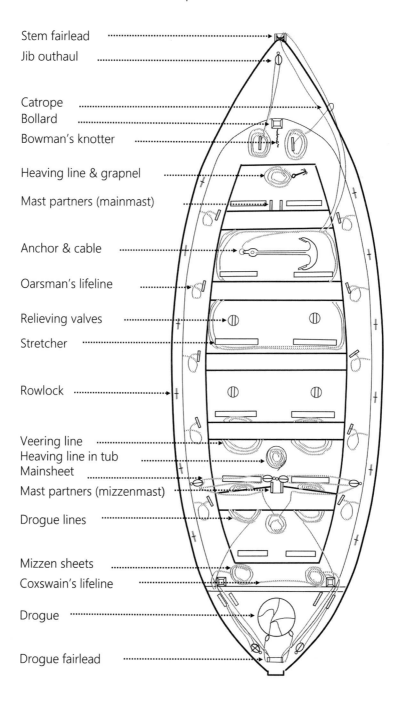

Stem fairlead

Jib outhaul

Catrope

Bollard

Bowman's knotter

Heaving line & grapnel

Mast partners (mainmast)

Anchor & cable

Oarsman's lifeline

Relieving valves

Stretcher

Rowlock

Veering line
Heaving line in tub
Mainsheet

Mast partners (mizzenmast)

Drogue lines

Mizzen sheets

Coxswain's lifeline

Drogue

Drogue fairlead

(Author's drawing based on a plan in Salcombe Maritime Museum)

The *William and Emma*: Construction Details

The *William and Emma* was a 35ft (10.66m) non self-righting lifeboat of the Liverpool type. Canadian rock elm was used for her keel and keelson, bilge keel, floors, gunwales and rudders. The stem and stern-post were of English oak. Honduras mahogany was used for the planking, bulkheads, decks, end boards and water ballast tanks.

A fragment of the hull from the *William and Emma* Lifeboat showing her double-diagonal planking with an oiled linen membrane sandwiched between. This gave great strength and a high resistance to leaking. *(Salcombe Maritime Museum)*

The planking was laid diagonally, the layers of the inner skin being reinforced by an outer skin arranged crosswise. Between these two skins of Honduras mahogany, there was a thick layer of stout unbleached calico, coated on both sides with a mixture of white lead and raw linseed oil. The skins were fastened with copper clench nails.

Short air chambers were fitted above deck at the bow and stern up to the gunwale and the whole of the space in the hold below deck was filled with wooden air cases to give buoyancy in the event of the boat being stove in. Ten self-acting non-return delivery valves were fitted to discharge, through the bottom of the boat, water taken on board. A solid cork fender, pear shaped, and covered with canvas, was worked round each side of the vessel. Two water-ballast tanks, each 16in (0.4m) wide, with a total length of 20ft (6m), were fitted in the centre line of the boat.

Two centre-boards, or drop-keels, each 9ft (2.7m) long, made of mild steel plate 5/16in (8mm) thick, having a drop of over 2ft (0.6m), were placed in steel trunks. Bilge keels were fitted on each side at the turn of the bilge, and hand battens were fitted on the bottom for the men to hold on by, should the boat capsize. When the *William and Emma* capsized in 1916, the crew tried to hold onto these battens but the power of the waves was so great that the men were swept away.

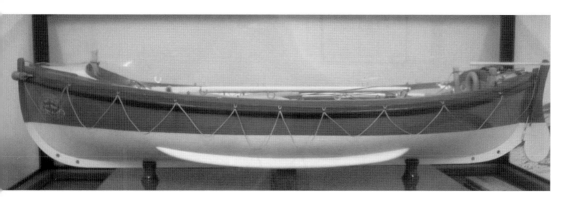

The *William and Emma* Lifeboat. Model by Mike Atfield in Salcombe Maritime Museum *(Salcombe Maritime Museum)*

the early hours of 4 August 1907 when the ketch *Bona* of Ipswich, was reported to be ashore off Prawle Point. Upon arrival at the scene, it was found that the *Bona* was under water, with her masts and sails still standing. There was no trace of the crew, so the lifeboat stood by until daylight when a search was made along the coast for the missing men. On returning to Salcombe it was learnt that the crew of the *Bona* had landed at Dartmouth in their own boat. On this and on other call-outs the lifeboat was reported to have behaved well.

The *William and Emma* had also performed well on practice launches in bad weather, so much so that her crew had complete confidence in her capabilities, saying of her 'that she would never hurt outside of the Bar'.

With the outbreak of war in 1914, a large number of young men from the Salcombe area, not already serving in the Royal Navy or in the merchant service, enlisted in the army and, by October 1916, many of those who had not volunteered had been conscripted. As a result, it fell to the older men in the town, or those exempted from service, to crew the lifeboat.

On 27 October 1916, when the *William and Emma* launched on her fateful mission, the average age of the fifteen men on board was 40. Sam Distin, the coxswain, was 47, his brother Albert, 49 and Peter Foale senior, the second coxswain, 56. Of the thirteen that perished, seven were born in East Portlemouth, although all lived in Salcombe at the time of the disaster. Many of the men were related. In addition to the two Distin brothers (Sam and Albert), there were the three Foales, Peter senior and his sons Peter, 35 and William, 32, and the two Cudd brothers Frank, 44, and Jack, 42. Some were related by marriage, others like Sam Distin and Thomas Putt worked together as fishing partners. Nine of the victims were fishermen or former fishermen and their loss was said to 'have practically wiped out the town's fishing fleet'.

The *William and Emma* was launched at Kingsbridge on 7 May 1904 after having been transported by rail from London. *(Fairweather Collection, Cookworthy Museum)*

The *William & Emma* on her launch day. The crew are stepping her masts prior to 'pulling and sailing' from Kingsbridge to Salcombe *(Fairweather Collection, Cookworthy Museum)*

Above: Two views of Salcombe Harbour in the early 1900s.
(Top: Salcombe Maritime Museum. Centre: Wyatt's Postcards)

Below: Extract from the 1927 Admiralty Chart showing the entrance to Salcombe Harbour
(Admiralty)

Both of the survivors, Eddie Distin, 25 (who was only distantly related to Sam and Albert Distin*) and Bill Johnson, 45, gave vivid first-hand accounts of the disastrous mission, either in evidence at the subsequent investigations or in rare interviews. Their accounts, together with the testimony of a key eye-witness, the Prawle Point Coastguard Chief Officer, Leonard May, are quoted at length in the narrative that follows.

---

* Sam and Albert Distin were Eddie's second cousins once removed. Their common ancestor was William Distin (1769-1837), Eddie's great, great grandfather.

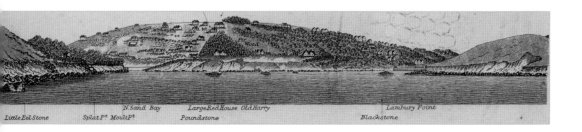

3   SHIP ASHORE!

In the early hours of 27 October 1916, severe southerly gales and heavy seas pounded the South Devon coast causing extensive damage. At Torquay, the Brixham fishing ketch *Girl Edith* had come ashore with the loss of her skipper and one of the crew and, in Start Bay, the crew of the *Traveller* of Fowey had been rescued after the schooner was driven ashore at Beesands Cellars. A number of other vessels were later reported missing at sea.

Up at the Prawle Point Coastguard Lookout, Chief Officer Leonard May had extra men with him on duty keeping 'foul weather' watch. Pitch dark, it was a wild, squally night, and some of the local telephone lines were down. At 5.12am, C.O. May observed a large blue light, a signal of distress, in the direction of the Meg Rocks, off Langerstone Point, just over half a mile to the east. Placing a man to watch for further distress signals, he sent another to rouse the rest of the crew from the Coastguard cottages below. A third man was instructed to call up Salcombe Coastguard by phone with the message: 'C.O. (Chief Officer) Prawle to S.O. (Senior Officer) Salcombe; signal of distress on Meg Rock, Langerstone Point.'

After making these arrangements, May signalled to the distressed vessel with a blue light to confirm that she had been spotted and to reassure her crew that help was on its way. He then made his way down the steep slope from the top of the Prawle Point headland to Langerstone Point, where he found the topsail schooner, *Western Lass* of Plymouth*, stranded in a sandy cove to the westward of Meg Rock – the only bit of sand in the vicinity.

Had she struck the Meg or 'Mag' nothing could have saved her, and the crew's only chance of rescue would have been by the lifeboat. Heavy seas were breaking over the schooner – her masts shaking as the waves struck.

Up at the lookout the coastguard officer tasked with phoning Salcombe was unable to get the message through until 5.50am because a section of the line was out of order. There was also a fault in the line to Lower House Farm in East Prawle where the lifesaving

A topsail schooner aground in a storm *(Salcombe Maritime Museum)*

The Coastguard cottages at Prawle Point in the 1920s *(Lloyd's of London)*

---

* The *Western Lass* was a 100 ton, two-masted schooner built in 1885 by William Hole Shilston at Coxside, Plymouth. Shilston retained ownership of her until 1907 when he transferred the vessel to his son Alfred. When she came ashore in the early hours of 27 October 1916 she was on a voyage from Swansea to Caen with a cargo of coal. Her master at the time is believed to have been W H Ellis. *Western Lass* survived her stranding and was sold to Albert Westcott of Plymouth on 15 January 1917. Her final end came ten years later when she was wrecked on the Brisons off Cape Cornwall on 13 July 1927. Fortunately her crew managed to row ashore.

Prawle Point Coastguard Station

The Coastguard Lookout at Prawle Point in 1922 *(Lloyd's of London)*

At the onset of the First World War, the Admiralty Coastguard Station at Prawle Point was designated a War Signal Station. From the Lookout at the top of the headland (Devon's most southerly point) Chief Officer May and his crew of nine men took it in turns to maintain constant day and night watch. They had a busy time of it signalling, with code flags, semaphore and flash lamp, to Royal Navy ships and reporting the movements of merchant ships. A telegraphist sent reports to the local naval command at Devonport and messages were passed to flanking Coastguard stations by telephone.

The Lookout, which is believed to have been built in the mid nineteenth century, had been in use as a Lloyd's Signal Station between 1883 and 1904, with civilian signalmen reporting the movements of both inbound and outbound ships to Lloyd's of London by telegraph. In 1903 the Admiralty took over Lloyd's signalling under contract and, with the lease of the old Coastguard station in East Prawle village about to expire, established a new station below the Lookout. The row of cottages was built in 1904-5 to house the chief officer, a petty officer, eight men and their families, together with the station office at the eastern end.

Lloyd's signalling ended in 1956. In 1983 a new base for the Prawle Point Coastguard Rescue Team was opened in East Prawle village and the old station closed. However, the Lookout remained in intermittent use until 1994. In 1997 volunteers from the National Coastwatch Institution (NCI) refurbished the building and today NCI watchkeepers serve as the Coastguards' 'eyes and ears' looking out for, and reporting, people and vessels in difficulty.

Langerstone   Meg
Point   Rock

The view east from
Prawle Point
Coastguard Lookout.
The *Western Lass* came
ashore at Langerstone
Point in total darkness
(Chester Wallace)

Prawle Point   Coastguard
Coastguard Lookout   Cottages

View from
Langerstone Point
looking west towards
Prawle Point and the
Coastguard Lookout -
now the National
Coastwatch Lookout
(Author)

apparatus was kept and so a messenger was despatched. After he arrived there at about 5.40am, the local volunteers, who formed the East Prawle Life Saving Apparatus Company, were summoned and the horses brought down from Town Farm to be harnessed to the rocket wagon.

Within minutes of the company's arrival at Langerstone Point at around 6.20am, the rocket apparatus was set up under the direction of Chief Officer May. With each man in his allotted place, the rocket was fired over the schooner's rigging. Attached to it was a continuous 500 yard (457m) length of line, the whip, which provided the means of passing a heavier line, the hawser, complete with the circular breeches buoy, out to the men on board. With the very first rocket they fired, the men of the lifesaving company got a line

The rocket line fired
over a stricken ship
*(internet image,
unknown source)*

The East Prawle Life Saving Apparatus Company

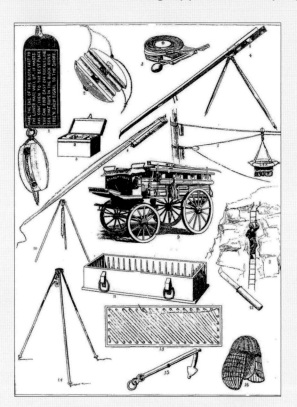

The Board of Trade Life Saving Apparatus

One of Chief Officer May's duties was to supervise the East Prawle Life Saving Apparatus Company – the forerunners of today's Prawle Point Coastguard Rescue Team. The company, made up of the regular Coastguard officers and between twenty and thirty local volunteers, was equipped with the Board of Trade Life Saving Apparatus. This was basically a horse-drawn wagon stocked with tripod, lights, rockets, breeches buoy, ropes and other essentials for rescuing crew and passengers from ships that had been wrecked close inshore. The rocket wagon was originally kept in the purpose-built Rocket House next to the old coastguard station in East Prawle, but at the time of the disaster it was housed in the linhay at Lower House Farm in the village. William Tucker of Town Farm supplied the horses.

The East Prawle Life Saving Apparatus Company was formed in 1878 and for one hundred years was to do sterling service. However, with the increased reliance on air -sea rescue helicopters, the company was disbanded in 1979.

across the stricken vessel and, once the hawser had been secured, the crew of the *Western Lass,* about five or six in number, were hauled safely ashore, one at a time, in the breeches buoy. The last man was landed at 6.52am.

Chief Officer May then despatched a messenger back to the coastguard station to inform Salcombe that the crew had been saved. The messenger reached the station at about 7.20am but he was unable to get through to Salcombe because the telephone was still not working properly. Apparently a branch of a tree had blown across the wires. Even if the message had got through it would have been too late, as the lifeboat had already been launched and was on its way to the scene of the wreck.

Breeches buoy rescue *(internet image, unknown source)*

A model of the *William and Emma* Lifeboat by Malcolm Darch in Salcombe Lifeboat Museum. The keel of the model is made from mahogany diagonal planking from the *William and Emma (Malcolm Darch)*

4 THE LAUNCH OF THE LIFEBOAT

Coxswain 'Big' Sam
Distin *(AE Fairweather)*

At Salcombe, the first warning that a ship was in distress had been received at 5.50am by the duty officer at the Coastguard Watchhouse at Orestone, near the Commercial Inn (now the Ferry Inn). A messenger was immediately sent to summon the lifeboat coxswain, Sam Distin who lived at 31, Buckley Street. In 1907 when, the *Bona* of Ipswich went on shore just off Prawle Point, the coxswain at the time, James Distin, Sam's elder brother, had rushed to Island Quay on receiving the alarm, to fire a maroon from the signal gun placed there. However, the gun had failed to fire, so he ran to the houses of the crew and launching party. It seems that 'Big' Sam had to do the same to rouse the men he needed. Perhaps the wind was blowing so hard that the maroons were not heard by those who were sleeping at the time. Or it may be that they were not fired in wartime, as was the case in the Second World War. James Cove's widow, Beatrice, recounted how her husband was roused by stones thrown at the window of their cottage in Robinson's Row, whilst Eddie Distin recalled a 'bang on the door':

> *Eddie Distin:* There was a bang on the door about a quarter past six in the morning and the coxswain Sam Distin shouted 'There's a ship ashore at Prawle. The boat's wanted. Rise and shine, Eddie.' Well, I got dressed, then ran out to the boathouse at South Sands. Well, ran and walked, it's a long mile to South Sands even going through The Moult grounds.

The lifeboat men and launchers as well as postmen and telegraph boys had permission to go through the grounds of The Moult. This route was fairly level compared with the alternative of going up North Sands Hill and then down again to South Sands.

> *Eddie Distin:* It was getting daylight, a right rough old morning, squally rain and blowing a full gale. When we got there we got rigged up in our oilskins and kapok lifejackets. There was big Sam Distin, the cox, and his brother Albert, Peter Foale senior, the second cox, his son Peter the bowman and his other son, William. There was Tom Putt, who had just left his wife in labour with their third child. He took a bit of stick from the lads like 'you'm better off with us than walking up and down the kitchen Tom'.

Doubts arose amongst the shore party as to whether the boat could get through the huge breakers on the Bar. The crew would have heard and seen the waves breaking on it as they made their way from the town to South Sands.

> *Eddie Distin:* Someone asked 'D'you think you'll get her out over [the Bar] skipper?' Sam replied 'No trouble and it will be a fair wind once we're over. Just you wait an' see'. Two of the crew were late so the cox shouted 'Who'll stand in then?' and, catching sight of Jack Cudd, who was an ex-naval man and the brother of Frank Cudd, one of the crew, 'What about it, Jack?' he asked. Cudd replied 'I'm with you.' Can't think who else was late, but there was James Cove, James Canham, Ashley Cook, Albert Wood, William Johnson and William Lamble.

William Lamble had arrived late but in time to take his place in the crew. Jack Cudd and Ashley Cook were standing in for the two regular crew members who either arrived too late or were unavailable that morning: Arthur Pedrick, a 37 year old fishmonger and

South Sands lifeboat house *(Salcombe Maritime Museum)*

The Salcombe Lifeboat
Lesty (1887-1904), with
crew and launching
party outside the South
Sands boathouse
*(Fairweather
Collection,
Cookworthy Museum)*

William March Distin, a 38 year old housebuilder and the brother of Sam and Albert.

The lifeboat was launched at 6.50am, one hour after the first warning of a ship in distress had been received at Salcombe and, unbeknown to the crew, just two minutes before the last man on the *Western Lass* had been rescued. With a full crew, and all her equipment on board, the *William and Emma* was hauled down the slipway by the launching team and into the water, in spite of the big waves that were looping round from the Bar into the small bay. Her water-ballast tanks were full, and each man wore his lifejacket.

Eddie Distin: In them days you needed about twenty launchers to get the boat out of the house, down the slip and across the sand into deep water because the boat was on a carriage with four big wheels. An' you had a pair of shafts just like an 'orse an' cart. You'd put a man in them shafts like an 'orse but wrong way round so he could guide the carriage into the water. It was all done backwards you see. The head launcher would get his men to move the boat out onto the slip, then call 'Right, all hands' and you'd clamber on board and sort yourself out. Then he would call 'Ready Cox?' The skipper would check that all were on board an' in their place, then reply 'Ready!' The pin [retaining the boat on the carriage] would be knocked out and off you'll'd go. 'Twas high water that morning*, an easy launch. We were away quickly.

News of the launch had spread throughout the town and people were already gathering on the track between South Sands and the Eelstone out towards Bolt Head, to watch the lifeboat fight its way over the Bar, and into the somewhat lesser dangers of the Range beyond.

William & Emma's successor, the *Sarah Anne Holden,* being guided down the slipway at South Sands *(RNLI)*

5 THE OUTWARD PASSAGE

A force 9 south-west severe gale reaching over 50 mph was hurling huge seas over the Bar. Propelling a boat with a laden weight of 6¼tons through the heavy surf called for a supreme effort on the part of the crew. Each oar weighed 25lbs (11.3kg). They were not all big men – James Canham and Ashley Cook, for instance were just 5ft 6ins (1.67m) tall and Cook weighed little more than 9 stone (58kg) – yet, collectively, the twelve oarsmen must have possessed tremendous strength. In 1874, former RNLI Secretary, Richard Lewis, in notes on the 'Management of Open Rowing Boats in a Surf', had written:

> Launching, and the initial effort of rowing to seaward, depends for its success on speed. Indeed, under some circumstances, safety will depend on the utmost speed being attained on meeting a sea. For if the sea be really heavy, and the wind blowing a hard onshore gale, it can only be by the utmost exertions of the crew that any headway can be made. The great danger is, that an approaching heavy sea may carry the boat away on its front, and then turn it broadside on, or up-end it, either effect being immediately fatal.

The *William and Emma*'s oars were painted white on the port side, and blue on the starboard and, because the rudder was ineffective at rowing speeds, the coxswain called out 'pull on your whites' and 'back your blues', in order to make the turn to starboard and face the breakers head-on.

---

* It was a spring tide with high water at 5.58am and low water just after noon. Sunrise was at 6.56am.

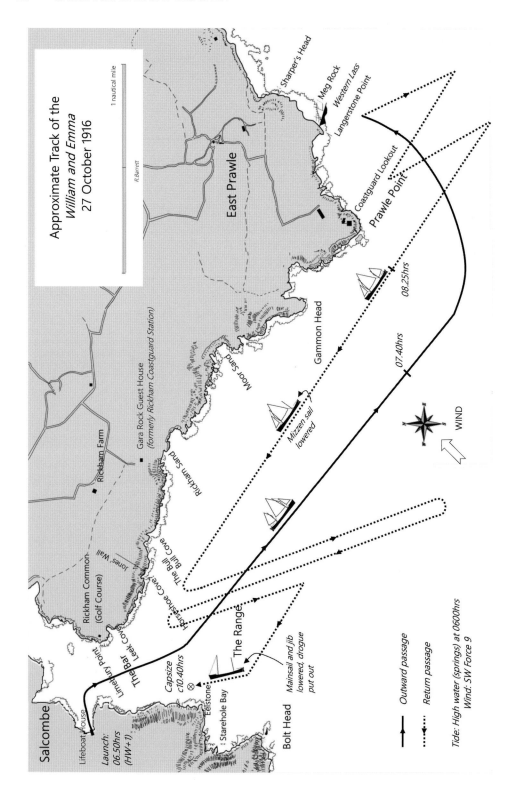

Approximate Track of the
William and Emma
27 October 1916

1 nautical mile

R.Barrett

Salcombe

Lifeboat House

Launch:
06.50hrs
(HW+1)

Limebury Point

The Bar

The Leek Cove

Capsize
c10.40hrs

Eelstone

Starehole Bay

Bolt Head

Mainsail and jib
lowered, drogue
put out

The Range

Horstone Cove

The Bull Cove

Rickham Sand

Moor Sand

Rickham Common
(Golf Course)

Jones' Wall

Gara Rock Guest House
(formerly Rickham Coastguard Station)

Rickham Farm

East Prawle

Gammon Head

Mizzen sail
lowered

07.40hrs

08.25hrs

Coastguard Lookout

Prawle Point

Langerstone Point

Western Lass

Meg Rock

Sharper's Head

WIND

Outward passage

Return passage

Tide: High water (springs) at 0600hrs
Wind: SW Force 9

When she was lined up, the twelve oarsmen took their timing from the starboard stroke and, keeping perfect rhythm, gathered speed before entering the surf – each one of them fully aware that a missed beat and a clash of oars could throw the lifeboat broadside on to the waves.

Those gathered on the shore watched with breathless anxiety as the lifeboat crashed through a breaker, disappeared into a trough beyond and then reared up again at an alarming angle to hit the following wave head on. Plunging through breaker after breaker, and then, shaking herself free, the lifeboat shaped a course south-eastward to Prawle, riding the waves 'like a little duck'.

> *Eddie Distin:* There was a very bad sea on the Bar, which was crossed under oars. We got out all right, no easy matter though. You had to have a good pair of hands to use those 'paddles'. They weren't light as you know. It took a while to battle our way out with tons of water breaking over us, but eventually we made it. When we got out over the Bar the skipper said 'Up sticks'. The drop keels were then lowered and after we put up the masts we put on the canvas. We had two reefs in the main, a reef in the fore and close-reefed mizzen. Away we went on a starboard tack straight for Prawle Point.

> *Bill Johnson:* There was never any hesitation about our ability to get over the Bar. We knew we could do that all right. We did. The boat, as a matter of fact, went out splendidly, though a little jumpily, because there was, no doubt about it, a very nasty sea. I have been going out in the lifeboat eighteen or nineteen years, and I don't remember any such weather.

Up at Prawle Point, Chief Officer May had returned to the lookout at 7.40am, after organising the rescue of the crew of the *Western Lass*. It was not long before he saw the lifeboat bearing approximately WSW on the starboard tack and heading about SE to clear the Point.

A Coastguard officer on watch at the Prawle Point Lookout
(NCI Prawle Point)

> *Chief Officer May:* The wind was blowing within a few points of a hurricane. The boat was splendidly handled, and was going like a greyhound and riding the waves beautifully. I had no day signal by which I could acquaint the boat that her services were not required. Had the incident happened at night I could have shown a green light. I did think of using the semaphore, but came to the conclusion that none of the

members would understand this method of signalling. [As a matter of fact, one of the crew – probably the ex-navy man, Jack Cudd – did]. Sometime later my attention was again called to the boat, and I realized that she had seen she was not wanted.

When the lifeboat was about two miles off Prawle Point the crew saw that the *Western Lass* was ashore and when they had got within about 1½ miles of the stranded vessel they realised that she was within reach of the rocket life-saving apparatus. Nobody could be seen onboard. Even if the distressed crew had still been aboard, the lifeboat would have been unable to approach near enough to render any assistance.

Eddie Distin: On rounding Prawle we saw the vessel in distress, a tops'l schooner. There was too much sea for us to get near the vessel and we couldn't see anyone on shore. But in fact the people had all got ashore before we had left home but the telephone lines were down and they couldn't get a message through. The sea had been getting worse while we had been out and we could see that we couldn't do anything. We hung around for a while then the skipper said 'That's it. Let's go home'.

Bill Johnson: We ventured inshore as far as we dared, and discovered that the crew could almost walk ashore, and were therefore not wanting any help from us. Finding we were not wanted we started to go back to Salcombe and, as there was no recall signal, continued on our way.

Waves breaking on Langerstone Point near where the *Western Lass* came ashore. The Prawle Point headland is in the background *(Author)*

Bolt Head   The Bar   Gammon Head

6   THE PASSAGE HOME

View from Prawle
Point looking west
towards Salcombe
Bar *(Author)*

To reach home the crew now had to sail into the teeth of the gale. As they tacked back conditions got worse, the wind increasing to near hurricane force. Prawle Point was weathered in about four tacks, the wind still the same.

> *C.O. May:* After a short tack to the southward, the lifeboat turned back and headed about north-west, perhaps a little to the windward, of north west. She would not weather Prawle Point on the second tack, but on the third, when it was about 8.25am she did so, and she made long legs for home.

> *Eddie Distin:* We had a terrible time trying to get back round Prawle with the sea really burying us down, but we were on our way home.

> *Bill Johnson:* As we sailed homeward the sea got worse, and we all got pretty wet from the heavy seas breaking over us.

Diagram of a Liverpool type lifeboat showing the two drop keels or centre plates. These greatly improved the boat's sailing qualities. They were lowered when the boat was sailing into the wind. To go about, the 'fore centre' would be lifted, allowing the bow to pay off more easily. *(RNLI)*

C.O. May: I saw her making good speed and good weather towards Salcombe Bar. Then rain intervened. She was alright at 10.20am but then we lost sight of her for a short while.

By this time crowds of people, including the wives and families of the lifeboat's crew, had assembled on the cliffs on the western side of the mouth of the harbour to watch the lifeboat combat the surging seas.

Eddie Distin: Just past Gammon Head [off Moor Sand] the skipper decided to take the canvas down. We lowered the mizzen but kept our course for the Bar.

When they were off Jones' Wall on the east side of Salcombe Range and in sight of the Bar, the crew saw how angrily the sea was breaking over it and discussed whether it would be better to make for Dartmouth.

Eddie Distin: The skipper said, 'What about it lads, are we going to give it a try?' Some said yes, others said no, so we turned out to sea away from the Bar thinking it was not fit to try.

The *William and Emma* stood off for about a couple of miles to give her sufficient sea room to clear the tidal races at Prawle and Start should it be decided to run for Dartmouth. However, before making that decision the cox stood in again to take another look at the Bar.

Eddie Distin: After going off two or three miles the coxswain said 'Wear round'. We did this, and came in a second time towards Jones' Wall. Again it was not fit to have a try. We wore round again and [to help the boat come round better] the skipper ordered us to 'Haul up the fore centre [plate]'. It came up to within six inches and then it jammed, but we lashed it there. It was not put down again as it was not wanted. The after centre was down and quite alright.

By now, the men had been in the boat for three and a half hours and the continuous drenching from the waves breaking over her was beginning to sap their strength. The prospect of a long haul round to Dartmouth and of being stranded there without sufficient money to get back home – a surprising, and no doubt undeserved, lack of confidence in Dartmothian hospitality – was not an inviting one. The weather was the same, the tide was nearly two hours before low water and the condition of the Bar appeared to have improved. The men had confidence in their boat and in themselves, and so they decided to attempt the crossing.

> *Eddie Distin:* About a half mile off the Bar, the skipper again said 'What do you think about it, boys, shall we try it?' By this time we were all pretty cold, wet and miserable and wanted to get home and the thought of having to go up to Dartmouth made most of us say yes.

> *Bill Johnson:* Some of the crew suggested, as we neared Salcombe, the advisability of not attempting to cross the Bar, but the majority had confidence that the lifeboat would prove equal to carrying us over; and as we were all, moreover, wet, had very little money in our pockets and anxious to get home, now so near, the verdict was given in favour of returning over the Bar to Salcombe. We saw, of course, how badly the sea was breaking over the Bar and realized that we should have need of all our seamanship to carry us over. The coxswain said 'We'll get her across a bit'. [In order to come over to the westward and cross the Bar by the deeper water passage that they generally used]. 'She will go in; she is bound to go in, never fear.' Then he said 'Lower away the mainsail'. Before we lowered the jib, he also said 'we'll put out the drogue and get everything in good working order'.

A drogue anchor – a hollow canvas cone towed astern to check the boat's way and keep her end on to the sea. *(Salcombe Maritime Museum)*

7   THE UNLUCKY WAVE

The boat was now near the Eelstone Rocks and heading straight for the Bar, which lay between a half a mile and a mile to the north. The drogue was out, the mainsail lowered, and the jib hauled down.

Then just as the crew were about to lower the masts and start the very dangerous row in through the huge seas that were breaking right across the harbour entrance, a mountainous wave suddenly towered up behind them and thundered over as it passed. Hitting on the port quarter, it lifted the stern high in the air and pitch-poled the lifeboat stern over bow.

The crew, all wrapped in stout oilskins and wearing lifebelts, were thrown into the boiling surf, but most managed to get to the over-turned hull and hang onto the hand battens and lifelines. Twice they were washed off by heavy waves, and each time fewer of them managed to scramble back. Then a bigger sea swept them all away and out of reach of the boat.

Eddie Distin. We had the jib in the boat and the halyards fastened when the coxswain sang out, 'Mind your life lines men'. That's when we met with the disaster. A bloody great sea struck us on the port quarter and pitch-poled us. That's tipped us end over end. We must have been almost a mile from the Bar when it happened. All fifteen of us got back on the bottom of the upturned hull [Eddie later said that he had found his way back by gripping the line of the drogue anchor] and I can remember the skipper saying to Bill Johnson 'What do you make of it Bill?' 'Not much Sam' Johnson replied. We got washed off two or three times and each time there was less of us who managed to scramble back. Then a bigger sea washed us off, and we couldn't get back again; it took us right away from the boat. It was impossible to swim, you just got rolled over and over and I did not see the boat again.

Bill Johnson. We took in the sails and put out the drogue, and were in the act of unshipping the mast and getting the oars out for the pull in when a tremendous sea struck and capsized the boat. We clambered on to her bottom, but were twice washed off, and each time I managed to grab and help a chum back. The coxswain looked to me and asked me what I thought of our chances, and I told him 'Not much'. Then we were all swept into the sea again.

The *Salcombe Times* reported that:

> With the boat torn from them and smashed up, lifebelts were of little avail in such an awful sea, and all, with the exception of Bill Johnson and Eddie Distin, were soon lost to view. Distin and Johnson owe their lives to a lucky accident. They happen to have been caught by a wave plunging shorewards, which lifted them up and hurled them many yards across the surface of the sea to rocks quite near the base of the cliffs, and to these fortuitous footholds they clung until rescued by persons who, having witnessed the catastrophe from the shore, had rushed to this particular spot, knowing from the run of the tide that here, if anywhere, the crew, alive or dead, must come ashore.

Bill Johnson: I remembered nothing after we were all swept into the sea again until I found myself on a rock some little distance from the shore, with Eddie Distin on another a few feet off. The waves broke over the rock and swished and swirled round it, but somehow I managed to hold on. Then the rescuers came, and of what happened subsequently I have only the haziest recollection. My watch stopped at 11.20am, so that must have been the time, I suppose, that we were thrown in the water.*

Eddie Distin's Watch which stopped at 11.03am. *(RNLI)*

The tumbling waves and the near hurricane force winds drove the capsized lifeboat for an hour against the ebb tide towards and eventually onto the rocky shore at Horseshoe Cove[†], east of Limebury Point, where it was reduced to a splintered mass of wreckage by the time the life-saving party had hurried there from Salcombe.

---

* Eddie Distin's watch stopped at 11.03am, whilst the watch found on Peter Foale junior's body, had stopped at 10.30am. C.O. May said that he saw the lifeboat capsize at 10.40am. Given that the local doctor, Dr Twining, was informed of the disaster about 10.45am whilst he was in town, 10.40am, or just a few minutes before, would appear to be the actual time of the fatal capsize.

† See footnote on page 42 regarding the location of Horseshoe Cove.

The Fatal Capsize 1

The *William and Emma* begins the run in. She has a drogue streaming astern
to steady her and the crew are about to lower the masts
according to laid-down procedure.

With a sudden roar a huge wave mounts high above the lifeboat and, becoming
unstable, begins to topple and then burst along her port quarter. Her stern is thrown
upwards as her bows bury deeply.

The Fatal Capsize 2

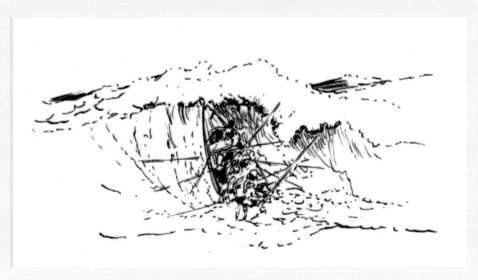

The lifeboat is pitch-poled and rolled over to starboard as the great wave engulfs
her. The crew are hurled forward – sweeps scatter like matchsticks.
The wave passes leaving devastation in its wake.

The capsized lifeboat is unsinkable but this is of little comfort to the struggling crew.
As often as they try to hang on to the lifelines and to the hand battens on the hull
they are swept away by successive, crashing waves. For an hour the capsized boat is
held between the hammering waves and the rushing tide. Despite their lifejackets,
one by one the survivors succumb to the waves until only two remain.

(Salcombe Maritime Museum)

Walter J Shaw's painting of the 'Unlucky Wave'. Shaw was a resident of Salcombe and witnessed the capsize of the lifeboat. *(Salcombe Maritime Museum)*

Another eye-witness picture. Entitled '*Salcombe Lifeboat Disaster (As seen One Minute before the Occurrence)*', it was painted by Salcombe photographer Edward Chapman. *(Edward Chapman)*

8 THE RESCUE OF THE TWO SURVIVORS

The news that the lifeboat had capsized immediately flashed through the town. Pitiful cries of distress were heard from those whose menfolk were in peril. Soon a party of men organized themselves into a lifesaving party with lifebuoys, ropes, stretchers and stimulants – Cyril Turner, the local lifeboat secretary, providing brandy and appliances. The men then got on the ferry boat* and crossed to the Portlemouth side. The strength of the current meant that they were unable to land at the usual place at Passageway. Instead they made for the Steamer Landing further upstream at Ditch End. They then raced a mile and a half along the coast path to Limebury Point, below Rickham Common, where they thought they might have a chance of giving aid to any survivors. After passing Limebury they found the splintered wreckage of the lifeboat, wedged into a small cove but, with no sign of the crew, they continued their search to the east.

Following hard on their heels was the local doctor, Dr Dan Twining. He had been walking through the town when, at about 10.45am, he was told that the lifeboat had been upset and the men had been seen clinging to her. He immediately rushed to his surgery to fetch the drugs he thought might be required and then crossed over to the Portlemouth side.

Strong and athletic, 31 year-old Dan Twining would have taken little time to cover the distance to Limebury. Before the Great War, he captained Blackheath Rugby Club and played rugby for Devon. In 1914-15 he served on the Western Front as a lieutenant in the Royal Army Medical Corps.[†]

Also rushing to join the rescuers was a party of men and nurses from Sharpitor VA Hospital on the Bolt Head side. From their viewpoint overlooking the Bar, a number of convalescent soldiers had seen the lifeboat capsize and quickly informed the Superintendent, Mrs Vereker, who, with her husband, was the owner of Sharpitor.

With the help of the Sister in Charge, Frances Vereker immediately set about organising a stretcher party. From the many volunteers, she selected five of her most able-bodied patients – Privates Mitchell, Doran, Taft, Jones, and Ford. Equipped with a stretcher, blankets, and

---

* This was a 20 foot, 2 cylinder motor ferryboat named *King George V.* It was introduced by Commander S W Ryder of the York Hotel in 1911. The regular ferryman was James Canham, but he was in the lifeboat on the day of the disaster.

[†] Dr Twining also served as the Medical Officer for Salcombe and the Commandant at Sharpitor VA Hospital. Sadly, he was severely disabled in a rugby accident after the war but he carried on serving the people of Salcombe until 1944. He died at Bideford in 1970.

Sharpitor VA Hospital

Nurses and convalescent soldiers at Sharpitor VA Hospital *(National Trust Overbecks)*

By the end of 1914, the casualties from the Western Front were so great that established hospital services were in danger of being overwhelmed. Accordingly the owners of many large houses, such as Sharpitor (now named Overbecks and in the care of the National Trust) lent them to the Red Cross for use as nursing or convalescent homes for treatment of the wounded. Known as VA or VAD (Voluntary Aid Detachment) hospitals, they were staffed by volunteers drawn largely from the middle and upper classes.

The owners of Sharpitor, George and Frances Vereker, gave up their home after their second son, 2nd Lieut Robert Vereker of the Grenadier Guards, was killed at Mons on the 25 August 1914, just twenty-one days into the war. Sharpitor VA Hospital opened on 23 August 1915, taking wounded 'Tommies', not officers, from hospitals at Exeter and Newton Abbot to complete their convalescence. Local people provided food, bedding and nursing help. They also entertained the patients, organising whist drives, billiard and rifle matches. By the time of Sharpitor's closure in 1919, 1,010 convalescent soldiers had passed through and, thanks to the dedication of the staff, not a single death was recorded. However, fifteen men departed with the addition of a bride from the neighbourhood!

medical supplies, the men were sent off to Salcombe with orders to get over the estuary to join the rescue party as fast as they could. They must have run 'like the wind' and (unless they crossed by motorboat) rowed 'like the devil' for it was reported that they reached Rickham Common in the remarkable time of thirty-five minutes. Following behind them was the Sister in Charge, Miss Allen, together with Sister Cocker and an orderly, Corporal Hathaway.

Back in Salcombe, the authorities tried to organise a rescue by boat but there were no craft in the harbour capable of making an attempt in such conditions. Lieut Albert Wilcock, the District Coast-watching Officer, did try and get down the harbour in the port patrol motor boat but had to turn back at the Bar. Conditions were too bad to launch the Hope Cove lifeboat *Alexandra* and the only remaining hope was for assistance from Plymouth, so John Vivian, Lloyd's sub-agent at Salcombe, telegraphed his opposite number at Plymouth asking him to seek help from the port authorities. Unfortunately no assistance was available, possibly owing to the state of the tide or the terrible weather.

Up at the Prawle Point lookout, Chief Officer May, having witnessed the capsize, gathered up rescue lines and equipment and set off with two of his men along the coast path in the hope of saving any of the crew that might have come ashore. Passing the Gara Rock Hotel (the former Rickham coastguard station which had closed just seven years before in 1909) they reached the vicinity of Jones' Wall – a distance of two and a half miles from Prawle Point. From there they saw Eddie Distin and Bill Johnson, clinging to a rock about forty feet from the shore.

> *Eddie Distin:* I was washed up on a big rock near Jones' Wall but clear of the mainland. And there was Bill Johnson. I hadn't seen him in the water and there we were side by side. We hung onto that rock like grim death because the sea was trying to wash us off again.

The two survivors had also been spotted by the Salcombe rescue party coming from the opposite direction, having walked and run the two miles along the coast path from East Portlemouth. With a great chasm of surging water between them and the two men, the rescuers soon realised that getting them ashore would be no easy task. Tom Perrett, a 43 year old Salcombe fisherman and professional yachtsman, took charge of the throwing lines and, assisted by others, scrambled down to the foot of the cliff. With the inrushing seas breaking around them, and after several fruitless attempts, Perrett managed to throw a thin line to Distin which he was able to grab hold of and secure.

By means of this line, brandy was sent across 'which had the effect of reviving the two men considerably'. Next a larger line was got to them. Johnson managed to secure this round himself and was hauled through the water to rocks on the mainland.

Eddie Distin: It was not long before someone was scrambling down the cliff and shouting to us to hang on. I don't know what they thought we were doing. Anyway a rope was thrown about twenty yards [18m] I suppose. I caught it with one hand while hanging on with t'other. Bill was getting on in years [at 45, he was 20 years older than Eddie] so I lashed in a bight and those ashore hauled him in while I steadied the rope. Some of the rescuers waded into the sea to try and save Bill as much as possible from the jagged rocks.

The same method was used to haul Eddie Distin across, but the arrangements did not work out so smoothly, as there was nobody to guide the rope for him as he had done for Johnson.

Eddie Distin: When it was my turn I had to lash myself up the best I could round my lifejacket and then jump. That's when I got knocked about pretty bad. The sea washed me onto the rocks and off again but they got me ashore in the end.

The location of Johnson and Distins' rescue. The photographs of the two men and the 'No. 4 view' at bottom left are from A E Fairweather's commemorative postcard on page 6 *(Fairweather Collection, Cookworthy Museum)*

W. JOHNSON   E. DISTIN

(Author)

1886 First Edition Ordnance Survey map, centred on NGR SX 743371

The Bull

(HM Ordnance Survey)

cliffs at ✕ in No 4 view. Johnson and Distin were rescued up the

Once at the base of the cliff, the two men were pulled out of the water, fastened to stretchers and hauled up the steep side to the top. By this time (between 11.30 and 12 o'clock) both Dr Twining and the nursing sisters from Sharpitor Hospital had arrived on the scene. The two nurses gave valuable assistance to Dr Twining by providing first aid care to Johnson and Distin, whilst one of the convalescent soldiers from Sharpitor, Private Ford, in a spirit of true altruism, stripped off his underclothes in spite of the cold weather to provide warm, dry clothing to wrap round one of the survivors.

The two men were then carried up to the pavilion of the Rickham Golf Links (owned by Richard Jordan of Gara Rock Hotel) and eventually to Rickham Farm, a large farmhouse on the Portlemouth side of the estuary – the home of Robert and Harriet Michelmore.

Eddie Distin: They took us to a shed (the golf pavilion) and I remember Dr Dan Twining asking if I wanted a fag which he gave me and a drop of lotion [brandy] too. [Two stimulants which are unlikely to be found in a doctor's medical case today!] Bill and I were very lucky. We were the only ones to be saved. Some of the bodies were washed ashore the same day, some later and two were never found. I was a fortnight at Rickham Farm. Johnson was there for longer. He never got over the disaster. He wouldn't go in a boat so they brought him back home by road via Kingsbridge. [It was Dr Cock, the Chairman of the local Lifeboat committee, who drove him home].

Rickham Farm in the
early 1900s
*(E. Chapman/National Trust
Overbecks)*

At Rickham, Johnson and Distin were treated with great care and compassion by Mrs Michelmore, assisted by her daughter Winifred, a VAD (Voluntary Aid Detachment) nurse, who had returned home the day after the disaster for the weekend. (The RNLI later expressed their gratitude to the Michelmores by awarding them an aneroid barometer). Also of great assistance was Norah Cunnington, a nurse who had been resting at Salcombe after many months of service in a French hospital nursing wounded soldiers from Verdun.

Both men were in a semi-conscious state when they were taken to Rickham and were still in bed and in considerable pain on the following Monday, when the first inquest took place. Bill Johnson had suffered extensive bruising after his buffeting in the sea, whilst Eddie Distin, in addition to bruising, was suffering from a nasty wound at the back of the head and cuts about his face. Distin was able to return home to Salcombe within ten days but Johnson was to remain at Rickham for over a month.

9 THE RECOVERY OF BODIES ON THE DAY OF THE DISASTER

Before Dr Twining reached the place where Distin and Johnson were brought ashore, he learnt that some bodies had already been found near Horseshoe Rock.* Going down to the rocks he saw the bodies of Peter Foale, senior, and Peter Foale, junior. Both had died of cardiac failure. They had been brought ashore by Tom Perrett and several other men in the rescue party, who, because the heavy sea was washing the bodies off to sea again, had to go into the water to recover them.

A little further out, among the breakers, Dr Twining could see Sam Distin. He was waiting for him to be brought in, when he got a message that another man had been brought in further along the coast. There he saw the body of William Foale, which had been found by Alfred Inch, a Salcombe boatman, just to the west of Horseshoe Cove. The body, which still had a lifebelt attached and was lying on the rocks with the sea washing all round, was taken up to the top of the cliff. On examination Dr Twining found that, like his father and brother, William had died of cardiac failure.

It was at this point that Dr Twining learnt that Eddie Distin and Bill Johnson had been brought ashore alive a little to the east, so he went off to attend to them. After seeing them carried safely up to the golf club pavilion, he next went to the place where Sam Distin's body had been brought ashore. Tom Perrett had found him in the water with his lifebelt over the shoulder, near to the body of Peter Foale, senior, between 11.30 and 12 o'clock. With Perrett was Sam Distin's brother, William, and together they hauled Sam's body out of the water and carried him up onto the cliff. As they were making their way up, someone above shouted that he was still alive, as he had seen him moving just before being taken out of the water. So attempts were made to resuscitate him – sadly without success.

---

* The author has been unable to establish the precise locations of Horseshoe Rock and Cove – the places where, in addition to the lifeboat wreckage, four bodies were said to have come ashore. The names are not marked on maps or charts and seem to have passed out of use. According to some local 'old salts', Horseshoe Cove is just to the west of Jones' Wall and The Bull. Confusingly, however, the only topographical features which match AE Fairweather's picture (on the following page), showing where the bodies of five of the crew were found, are just to the east of Leek Cove. It was here that one local resident remembers being shown, as a child, the place where bodies were found. The body of Ashley Cook is known to have been found at Leek Cove and Fairweather's reference to five bodies must relate to Ashley Cook together with Sam Distin, Peter Foale and his two sons, as the remaining bodies were found near Gara Rock and in the estuary (see map opposite and on page 49).

The 'No. 3 view' in AE Fairweather's contemporary postcard (see page 6). The caption reads 'the bodies of five of the crew were found soon after the accident on the rocks of No. 3 view'.
(AE Fairweather)

When Dr Twining arrived, he pronounced him dead, partly as a result of asphyxiation, caused by a large quantity of water having got into his lungs. Sam Distin's body and those of Peter Foale and his two sons were carried over the golf links to the coach house at Manor Farm, Rickham.

In the afternoon, between 4 and 5 o'clock, another body was found floating, complete with oilskin and lifebelt, on the Portlemouth side in the water below the Passageway (near the ferry landing). It had been spotted by the ubiquitous Tom Perrett while crossing the harbour on the ferry. The body, later identified as that of Frank Cudd, was lifted into the ferry-boat, and taken to a yacht owned by a Dr Fenton. Dr Twining's subsequent examination found that Frank Cudd's neck had been broken, probably by the lifeboat and that his death would have been instantaneous.

Seven of the fifteen man crew – two survivors and five dead – had now been accounted for. In the days that followed, local people kept up a constant vigil for the remaining eight.

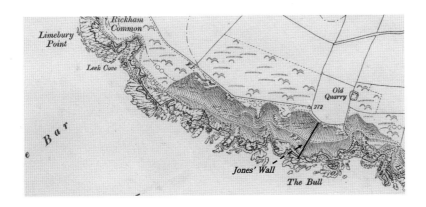

Extract from the 1907 Ordnance Survey map showing the coast east of Limebury Point. The location of Jones' Wall has been added.
(Ordnance Survey)

10   A TOWN IN MOURNING

As the extent of the disaster became clear, the small community of Salcombe was plunged into a state of shock. The town was no stranger to grief and loss – sixteen of its sons had already given their lives in the Great War, whilst losses at sea had been commonplace in the days when the town was home to a great fleet of sailing ships. Yet no one could remember a time when so much sorrow had entered so many homes at one blow. The local newspaper described Salcombe as a 'town in mourning':

> With the disaster that occurred to the Salcombe lifeboat on Friday, the members of the crew were in sight of home, and many members of their families were watching their loved-ones gallantly fight against the elements to once again reach the safety of the harbour. The agonising sight of watching their husbands and brothers battling for their lives, and have to patiently stand on the cliffs and watch the cruel sea become victors, and later in a few cases, to see the bruised remains cast up by the waves, can only be imagined and not described.
>
> The disaster has plunged Salcombe, usually sunny and smiling, in profoundest grief and sorrow, and not the less poignant because the times have more or less familiarised us all with death. It has become a town of mourning. Yet the suffering is borne silently behind closed doors, and traceable in the streets and business premises only in the sober faces and quiet demeanour of the people.
>
> Persons whose lives had not been cast in the restricted grove of a tiny town can have little or no conception of how terrible a vehicle of grief not only to the mothers and wives and children of the lost, but to the whole population, is a catastrophe of such magnitude in Salcombe. The same, or an even greater number of men might die in the faithful discharge of duty, as these men did, in some big town and their fellow-townsmen dismiss the subject with a mere expression of pity. In Salcombe it is different. The families of the working classes are connected to a degree which does not obtain in bigger centres of population, one with another, by all the ramifications of relationship by marriage and birth; but even beyond that the whole community, inter-dependent as they are one on another for the means of life and society, is knit together in a very real brotherhood. Everybody knows everybody else,

Fore Street, Salcombe
(Salcombe Maritime Museum)

and even between the fishermen and the people who live in the big houses there is, without any forfeit of respect, a link of friendship and familiarity which leads the professional or independent gentleman to greet his poorer neighbour as 'Sam' or 'Tom'. These being the conditions of daily life there is sadness not only in the homes of the lost lifeboat crew, but in every house in Salcombe.' *(Salcombe Times)*

11   AFTERMATH: THE EVENTS OF THE FOLLOWING FORTNIGHT

In the days that followed, furious storms continued to lash the coast, hampering efforts to find the remaining eight crew members. In Salcombe normal life came to a standstill as the townsfolk continued the search, supported the grief-stricken families and attended a grim succession of inquests and funerals.

Saturday, 28 October. Reports of the disaster appeared in newspapers throughout the country and two local papers, *The Western Daily Mercury* and *The Evening Herald*, launched an appeal on behalf of the dependants of the men who had lost their lives.

Between 9 and 10 o'clock in the morning, Walter Harding, a master mariner, from Portlemouth, and five other men found the body of Ashley Cook, jammed between the rocks at Leek Cove, east of Limebury Point, and carried him up to Rickham Farm.

That night, Edith Putt, still in a state of shock at the loss of her husband, gave birth to a son, Thomas Henry.

Sunday, 29 October. Dr Twining examined Ashley Cook's body and confirmed the cause of death as cardiac failure.

In the morning service at Holy Trinity Church, the Vicar, Rev J A Sidgwick, who had been out on the rocks two days before with the rescue party, said:

Edith Putt, Thomas Putt's widow
(Lin Morrissey)

We have come together today under the cloud of a great disaster. Our minds are filled with distressing thoughts of the sad calamity which has fallen so suddenly and swiftly upon our little town. Bound on an errand of mercy, these brave men faced the perils of the sea in order to rescue others who were in danger, and we know with what result to themselves. It leaves us dazed, stunned, and perplexed. We cannot understand it. It is too hard for us ... In the sanctuary of God, in prayer and communion with Him, may we find the help and comfort that we need.

Monday, 30 October. An inquest was held in the Council Hall by Thomas Edmonds, the deputy coroner for Devon. Aaron Dornom, a respected local boatbuilder and former lifeboatman, was appointed foreman of a jury made up of local men. Their first task was to ensure that the six bodies, which had been brought across the estuary to the mortuary in the town's cemetery, were formally identified. After visiting the mortuary the jury heard evidence from relatives of the deceased as well as from the men who recovered the bodies. Their identities were confirmed as follows:

Frank Cudd, identified by his brother, Norman Cudd, a Royal Navy Petty Officer.

Peter Foale and his sons, Peter and William, by the only remaining son, Cecil, a merchant sailor, living at 7, Orestone, Salcombe.

Samuel Distin by his son, Gunner John Henry Distin, (Royal Garrison Artillery) of 31, Buckley, Salcombe.

John Ashley Cook by his father, John Henry Cook, of Council Quay, Salcombe, a pleasure boat proprietor.

In giving evidence John Cook said that his son was not a recognised member of the lifeboat crew and that he did not know he was going into the boat. In fact he had sent for him to come and help him as one of his boats had broken adrift.

As to the causes of the accident, the Coroner raised the question of the boat not being a 'self-righter' and whether the crew might have been saved if she had been. Responding on behalf of the RNLI, Lieutenant Keppel Foote, the acting deputy Chief Inspector of Lifeboats, said that the choice of lifeboat had been left to the Salcombe crew, who, six or seven years ago were given the opportunity of inspecting and testing the different boats in use. James Distin (brother of Samuel Distin), who was coxswain at the time when the *William and Emma* was selected, said that their previous boat had been a self-righter, but the non self-righting boats were more roomy and better sailers. Finally, one of the jurors, Thomas Elliott, a yacht skipper, claimed that 'You would never be able to work the self-righting boat in all winds over the Bar'.

The Coroner concluded that 'there appeared to be no blame attached to anyone. The crew very gallantly went to sea, with every confidence in their boat, but a big wave came and capsized her'. The verdict of the jury was that 'the men lost their lives by the capsizing of the lifeboat'.

Letters and telegrams of sympathy were now 'pouring in' from all over the country and, just after the inquest closed, a telegram was received in Salcombe from the King:

The Council Hall in Market Street where the inquests were held – now the home of the Tourist Information Centre and the Salcombe Maritime Museum *(Salcombe Maritime Museum)*

I am concerned to hear of the distressing accident to the Salcombe lifeboat whereby thirteen of her brave crew have lost their lives in attempting to save others. Please convey my sympathy to the families of the gallant men who have perished. GEORGE, R.I. (King George V)

The message had been received by the Chairman of the RNLI, Lord Waldegrave and passed on to the local RNLI Secretary, Cyril Turner. Lord Waldegrave in his reply to the King said:

I humbly thank your Majesty on behalf of the Royal National Lifeboat Institution for your gracious message of sympathy, which I have conveyed to relatives of the gallant men who lost their lives in the Salcombe lifeboat disaster while engaged in attempting to rescue a shipwrecked crew, thus carrying out the noble traditions of the lifeboat service.*

Although the community was still stunned by the disaster, great efforts were now being made to rally round those who had lost their love ones and alleviate their suffering. With so many wishing to contribute, a local committee was formed to organise a distress fund. Based largely on the local RNLI committee, its chairman was Dr William Cock and secretary, Mr. Cyril E Turner. (The RNLI later showed their 'appreciation of the valuable and indefatigable assistance rendered by Dr Cock and Cyril Turner' by according them the Thanks of the Institution, Inscribed on Vellum and framed).

At a national level, the Lifeboat Institution confirmed that it would meet the cost of burial of each member of the crew and pay annuities to their families for the time being. Of the thirteen men who lost their lives, eight had wives and, between them, they left behind eighteen children aged under 16.

Tuesday, 31 October. The funerals of Peter Foale and his two sons took place in the afternoon, with flags in the town flying at half-mast and all the business premises closed. Walking with the mourners – Mrs Foale, her only remaining son, Cecil, and her daughters – were the relatives of other members of the crew who had lost their lives. A large congregation, which included representatives of many local organisations, attended the service in Holy Trinity Church.

Holy Trinity Church, Salcombe
(Wyatt's Postcards)

* The RNLI had not suffered such a loss since the Kingstown (now Dún Laoghaire) lifeboat capsized in 1895 with the loss of all 15 of her crew. The worst disaster in RNLI history had been in 1886 when the Southport and Lytham St Annes' lifeboats lost 14 and 13 men respectively in the *Mexico* disaster. Since 1916 only one other disaster has taken a greater toll than that suffered at Salcombe. That was in 1928 when the Rye lifeboat capsized with the loss of all 17 of her crew.

John Ashley Cook's
gravestone in
Shadycombe Cemetery
(Author)

Wednesday, 1 November. The local community again turned out in large numbers for the funerals of Sam Distin, Ashley Cook and Frank Cudd. Two funeral services were held at Holy Trinity Church, conducted by the vicar, the Rev J A Sidgwick. In the case of Ashley Cook, the Rev J Wilfred Dunstan, the Wesleyan minister, read the committal and the prayers at the cemetery, the vicar pronouncing the benediction. It was a busy day for the vicar, for it was All Saint's Day and, in addition to the three funeral services at the church and cemetery, he conducted three more services in the parish that day.

Thursday, 2 November. Albert Distin's body was recovered. It had been found in the morning by John Elliott, a farmer from High House, East Portlemouth, at Rickham, near Gara Rock and had apparently been left by the tide the night before, with the rising tide just about to reach the body again.

In London, a special meeting of the Lifeboat Institution's Management Committee agreed to make a grant of £2197 to the relief fund, in addition to the payment of funeral and medical expenses and a sum of £75 for the immediate relief of the dependants.

Friday, 3 November. Following the recovery of Albert Distin's body the day before, a second inquest was held at the Council Hall in the evening. The jury was the same but on this occasion the inquest was presided over by the County Coroner, Sidney Hacker.

The identity of the disfigured body lying at the mortuary was confirmed by William Distin, who recognised his brother, Albert, from the shape of his ears and hands, and by a tattooed ring on a finger.

Turning to the cause of the accident, the foreman, Aaron Dornom, said there were rumours that some of the fittings of the boat were not in proper order and of the drop keels not being right. This view was contested by Dr William Cock, the Chairman of the Lifeboat Committee (as well as the Urban District Council), who said that the drop keels were in perfect working order when he went out in the lifeboat on an exercise the previous month. The keels were used for sailing and he could not understand, even if both were down, how it would affect the accident.

At this point one of the jurors asked that the survivors be called to give evidence but Dr Twining stated that the two men were suffering from severe strain and exposure so would not be able to appear for at least a week.

The jury then returned the verdict that Albert Distin's death 'was due to drowning through the capsizing of the lifeboat'.

The Coroner then asked the jury to sit again, as the body of another victim had been found that day washed a considerable way

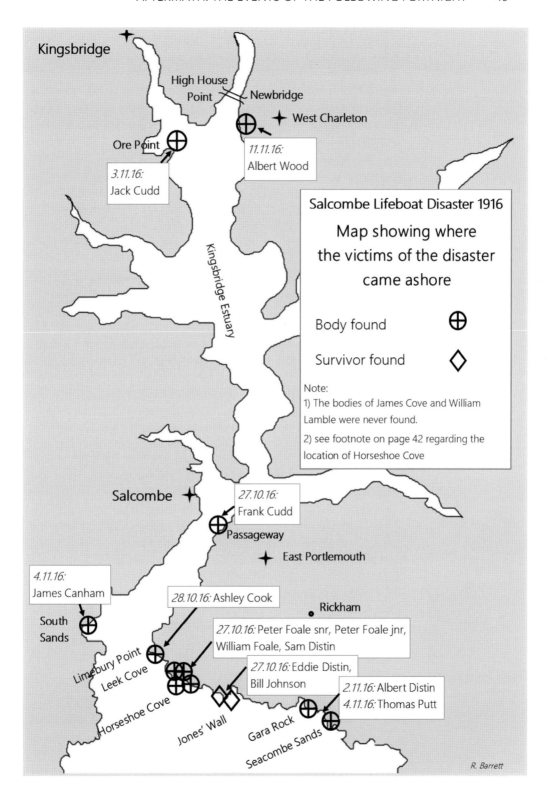

Kingsbridge

High House Point — Newbridge

West Charleton

Ore Point

11.11.16:
Albert Wood

3.11.16:
Jack Cudd

Kingsbridge Estuary

Salcombe Lifeboat Disaster 1916

Map showing where the victims of the disaster came ashore

Body found ⊕

Survivor found ◇

Note:
1) The bodies of James Cove and William Lamble were never found.

2) see footnote on page 42 regarding the location of Horseshoe Cove

Salcombe

27.10.16:
Frank Cudd

Passageway

East Portlemouth

4.11.16:
James Canham

28.10.16: Ashley Cook

Rickham

27.10.16: Peter Foale snr, Peter Foale jnr, William Foale, Sam Distin

27.10.16: Eddie Distin, Bill Johnson

2.11.16: Albert Distin
4.11.16: Thomas Putt

South Sands

Limebury Point

Leek Cove

Horseshoe Cove

Jones' Wall

Gara Rock

Seacombe Sands

R. Barrett

up the creek towards Kingsbridge floating in shallow water at Ore Point. It was discovered by Fred Ford, a painter from Kingsbridge.

The body was identified by Norman Cudd as that of his brother, John (Jack) Ambrose Cudd (Norman Cudd had already appeared at the first inquest to confirm the identity of his other brother, Frank). There was no clothing on the body, but a tattoo mark on the arm confirmed his identity.

The inquest jury returned the same verdict as before – death due to drowning through the capsizing of the lifeboat – and went on to express their thanks to the many willing helpers who went to the rescue, making special mention of the services of Thomas Perrett, whose experience in 'manipulating the lines' had proved invaluable and without whom 'it is possible that there would have been no survivors'. (Tom Perrett was also responsible for recovering four of the bodies). In addition, the jury expressed their appreciation of the services of Nurse Cunnington who had helped the Michelmores nurse the two survivors at Rickham.

Saturday, 4 November. The bodies of James Canham and Thomas Putt were recovered in the morning. That of Jim Canham, the ferryman, was found by a local resident, Mr Lionel Jackson, at South Sands, lying on the lifeboat slipway. It must have been left by the tide on Friday night and, by a strange twist of fate, returned by the sea to the very place from where Canham and his crewmates had embarked on their fateful mission a week before. On the day before he died, one of his ferry passengers, who later described him as 'poor Canham, the nice ferryman', remarked on the day's unseasonably warm and sunny weather, to which he had made the prophetic reply 'yes, but we shall have to pay for it.'

Thomas Putt's body, lying some distance away on Seacombe Sands, Rickham at high water mark, was found by John Elliott, the farmer from High House, East Portlemouth who had found Albert Distin's body two days before.

An appeal letter, signed by the Chairman of the local Committee, Dr William Cock, and the Secretary, Cyril Turner, published in the November 4th edition of the *Salcombe Times,* stressed the need for a substantial fund to support the families of the deceased.

The lifeboat house and slipway at South Sands
(Edward Chapman/ Bangwallop)

> The crew consisted chiefly of fishermen, and they were all hard-working men who had earned the respect of their neighbours. Unfortunately the men who were lost have not been able to make adequate provisions for their wives and families ... We cannot recall the men who have been lost, but we must try to alleviate the sorrow of their relatives by raising a substantial fund, to prove that the brave conduct of the crew is appreciated by their fellow countrymen. Eight of the

men who were drowned left widows, and as far as we can ascertain the total number of other dependants is twenty.

Sunday, 5 November. The funerals of Albert Distin and John Cudd took place despite the extremely stormy weather. The *Salcombe Times* reported that:

> The same fellow townsmen and representatives of Institutions and Societies again wended their way to the graveside to do honour to the gallant dead. The coffins were borne into church together, and the Vicar, the Rev J A Sidgwick, conducted the service in church and at the graveside. It almost seemed as though there was a more representative attendance from the outlying villages than that at the funerals of those [of the crew] that had previously been interred. On each coffin there was a very large number of beautiful floral tributes.

In the evening, a Memorial Service was held at the Wesleyan Church. Addressing a large congregation, the Rev J Wilfrid Dunstan said:

Albert Distin's gravestone in Shadycombe Cemetery *(Author)*

> We are gathered together tonight in the saddest of circumstances. Salcombe has received the severest blow in the history of the town. Ten homes have been stricken, but when we remember the intermarriages in small places, it is easier to understand the extent of the grief. War has its casualties and we expect them; but sorrows attending the service of Love are heart breaking ...
> Nothing is more heroic than the service they rendered. Before them, the angry billows, screaming in awful fury, mighty waves towering high and threatening to engulf any who venture to combat them. They do not go forward to meet a mortal foe, their antagonist is the hungry, devouring, never satisfied sea. It is a brave heart that ventures to battle with such a grim monster. It was a high conception of Duty which compelled one of the crew to say, when urged by loved ones to resign his position in the lifeboat crew, 'I cannot, with my knowledge of the coast. It is my duty to man that boat'. Such men are heroes indeed.

Monday, 6 November. Following the recovery of the two bodies on Saturday, the County Coroner, Sidney Hacker, conducted another inquest. Alfred E Cook identified his brother-in-law, James A Canham and James A Friend, his step-father, Thomas Putt.

The jury had again asked if the two survivors could be called and so the Coroner sent a constable to consult Dr Twining but he was not at home. Bill Johnson was still recovering at Rickham Farm and, although Eddie Distin was back at home, Mrs Distin said he could not leave the house without permission from the doctor. The Coroner accordingly adjourned the inquest to the following Monday.

Tuesday, 7 November. The Wesleyan Church was packed again when the Rev J Wilfrid Dunstan conducted the combined funeral service for James Canham and Thomas Putt. James' daughter Doris, only four years old at the time, remembered wearing a purple dress and throwing violets onto her father's coffin.

Wednesday, 8 November. The solemn atmosphere prevailing in the town was described in a letter written by a Salcombe lady to her daughter:

> There has been an awful gloom over the place for some days. When I went out I never saw a soul, the whole place seemed deserted; [the men were] all over the other side, watching and searching. The normal state of things is beginning to come back now men are at work again.
>
> Oh! It has been terrible, such constant anxiety, everyone on the rack all the time. Three of the men are still missing. Poor Canham, the nice ferryman, was found on the slope of the lifeboat house and was buried only yesterday. I'm afraid there is no hope of finding the others now. They were so dashed about on those cruel rocks.

Thomas Putt's gravestone in Shadycombe Cemetery
(Author)

Island Street, Salcombe with the Wesleyan Chapel on the left
(Fairweather Collection, Cookworthy Museum)

James Canham, steering the *King George V* motor ferry before the disaster (*Fairweather Collection, Cookwarthy Museum*)

Albert Distin was the one that saved the son of the man who had the yard opposite and the other, the cox, was the big fisherman who had the boats just outside here and used to pace up and down. He and his partner Putt both gone. They have just put his boat up into the yard today. Poor fellows, we shall miss them. Johnson (saved) is the red bearded man who used to hold forth so much and advise everybody about everything. He is terribly knocked about and not able to be moved yet. I saw Mrs Michelmore this morning and she says he has only been out of bed for ten minutes yet. Ashley Cook is Florence's eldest brother; Bert Wood, the only son of Mrs Wood at the little baker's shop, nephew of Mrs Banthorpe. Cove was the man Colonel Cromie had [to take him fishing] while he was here, a nice man. It is practically all the fisher-men gone.

They have got a lot of money for the women, there are eight widows and twenty dependants. The Lifeboat Association will do something handsome, they say £2000, but I shouldn't think so much. Poor Mrs Putt had a baby the day after and Mrs Distin is expecting one every day. It is awful for them.

It has been a terrible time, one storm after another. Men who have been in India say they never saw it rain harder than we have had it once or twice. Three nights I've been up nearly all night and last Saturday I think the worse. All the boats outside here were swamped and nothing but a sheet of foam to be seen when I got up on Sunday morning. The high tide was all over the Quay.

Saturday, 11 November. A retired railway clerk, R J Sharatt, who lived at Kingsbridge, found the body of Albert Wood when he went for a walk over New Bridge (on the main road to West Charleton) in the morning. Crossing the bridge he went along the shore and, near the Mill Lime Kiln at Charleton, saw a body lying at the high water mark. He returned quickly to Kingsbridge and informed the police, who later removed the body to the Salcombe Mortuary.

Tennyson's *'Crossing the Bar'*

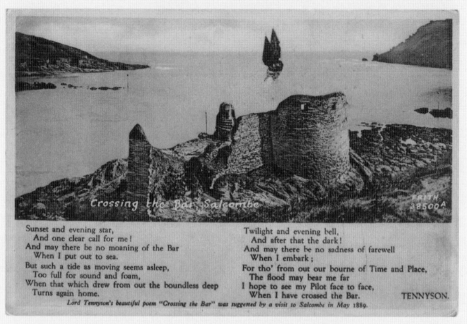

Sunset and evening star,
  And one clear call for me!
And may there be no moaning of the Bar
  When I put out to sea.
But such a tide as moving seems asleep,
  Too full for sound and foam,
When that which drew from out the boundless deep
  Turns again home.

Twilight and evening bell,
  And after that the dark!
And may there be no sadness of farewell
  When I embark;
For tho' from out our bourne of Time and Place,
  The flood may bear me far
I hope to see my Pilot face to face,
  When I have crossed the Bar.   TENNYSON.

Lord Tennyson's beautiful poem "Crossing the Bar" was suggested by a visit to Salcombe in May 1889.

(Fairweather Collection, Cookworthy Museum)

Salcombe Bar is believed to have inspired Lord Tennyson's famous poem *'Crossing the Bar'*. Written in 1889, three years before Tennyson died, the poem is a metaphor for crossing into an afterlife with the Bar representing the barrier between life and death.

At the Memorial Service for the lifeboat victims, held at Holy Trinity Church on 5 November 1916, *'Crossing the Bar'* was sung by the choir to Woodward's setting. In his sermon, the Rev Wilfrid Dunstan referred to Tennyson's visit to Salcombe, twenty-seven years previously. He said that one of the victims of the disaster, Peter Foale senior, was the pilot that took the poet laureate safely across the Bar in Lord Brassey's famous yacht the *Sunbeam*. 'At the time the church bells were ringing for evensong and as the yacht crossed the Bar, the seas became angrier and rushed across to the harbour mouth with a hollow moaning sound.'

(The poem, set out in the postcard above, is reproduced in larger print on page 76)

Monday, 13 November. When the inquest, which had been adjourned the previous Monday, resumed in the afternoon it now had three victims to consider: James Canham and Thomas Putt who had already been buried and Albert Wood whose body was identified by his father, Edwin Wood.

Giving evidence for the first time was Eddie Distin. He said that the capsize was due to 'an unlucky and huge wave, which struck the boat and turned her end over end'. When asked by the coroner to confirm that the accident was caused by the terrible weather and nothing else, he simply responded, 'Yes'. Distin went on to praise the skill with which the lifeboat had been handled, and said that the accident had destroyed none of the confidence he had in the boat, 'She was a splendid boat, and we shall have a job to get a better one. We never shall.'

When asked about the jamming of the forward drop-keel he said that this had occurred just before they tried to re-cross the Bar and they couldn't get it back all the way into the centre case. However, he was insistent that it had nothing to do with the accident. The Foreman, Aaron Dornom, asked him if the coxswain had made any remark about the plate jamming, to which he replied 'No, none.'

Once again the verdict of the jury was that the men lost their lives by the capsizing of the lifeboat.

Tuesday, 14 November. Business premises were again closed and blinds drawn throughout the town for the funeral of Albert Wood. The service was conducted by the Wesleyan Minister, the Rev J Wilfred Dunstan and was again very well attended.

This was to be the last of the funerals as the bodies of James Cove and William Lamble were never found. James Cove is nevertheless commemorated in Shadycombe Cemetery on the headstone which marks the grave of his son Henry, who died in 1939, and his wife, Beatrice Anne, who died in 1962, aged 80. Although Beatrice survived her husband by 46 years, she was apparently so traumatised by his loss that she turned deaf and rarely left her home.

Of the eleven disaster victims buried in Shadycombe Cemetery, the graves of all but one are marked with a headstone. Sam Distin was buried in an unmarked grave.*

Seven weeks after the disaster, on Sunday 17 December, large numbers of townsfolk attended a memorial service at Salcombe Church for James Cove and William Lamble.

James Cove with his wife Beatrice and three of his four children: Viola, Henry and Mary
(Diana Brown)

---

* Salcombe UDC burial records list the plot number as Section 11, no. 138

12   THE RELIEF FUND

By the end of the year, a total of £10,759 had been raised by donations from home and abroad. (Approximately £654,000 at today's values). The money was collected or subscribed as follows:

Local Committee	£2889
Royal National Lifeboat Institution	£2135
Western Daily Mercury & Western Evening Herald	£2399
Members of and subscribers to Lloyd's	£2600
Mr Andrew McIlwraith from ship owners and others	£735

Of the total, £5000 was invested in 6% Exchequer bonds and £5300 in a 5% War Loan. Following approval by the Charity Commissioners, five trustees were appointed to administer the Salcombe Lifeboat Fund. One was the then Secretary of the RNLI, George Shee, the others were local men: Dr William Cock MRCS, LFCP of Hazeldene; Mr Andrew McIlwraith of Woodcot, shipowner; Mr Ernest Capel Cure, of the Grange, member of Lloyd's, and Mr Cyril Edward Turner, solicitor.

The trustees were given authority to spend up to £100 on a permanent memorial to the thirteen men who died (this was later contributed to the town's War Memorial Fund) and to make one-off payments of £100 to Bill Johnson and £50 to Eddie Distin to settle any claims the two survivors might make for their injuries. As Albert Wood left no dependants, his father was granted £50.

The eight widows (as well as William Wakeham's dependent mother and James Canham's mother-in-law) each received £1 1s 0d (£1.05p) a week, or, if they remarried, 10s 6d (52½p) a week for their remaining years. By time the first payments were made, the number of dependent children aged under 16 had reduced from eighteen to thirteen. The eldest in each family received four shillings (20p) a week until he or she reached 16, the second child, three shillings (15p), and the remaining children, two shillings (10p) a week each. When an elder child died, or reached the age of 16, the younger siblings each received an extra shilling (5p) a week (up to the maximum of four shillings). Florence Foale and Emily Canham (the grown-up daughters of Peter Foale senior and James Canham) both suffered from epilepsy, so they received a weekly allowance of 7s 6d (37½p) as long as they remained unmarried.

As the years went by, a degree of resentment grew up amongst some of the bereaved families because of the provision that surplus funds could be transferred to the RNLI if the residue was sufficient to meet all the commitments to the dependants. Some took the view that the money had been specifically donated by well-wishers for

Particulars of Dependants of Men
who lost their Lives.

JOHN ASHLEY COOK, 49, Fore Street, Salcombe.
Fisherman. Married. Age 24.
Wife age 23.
Two Children (boy age 2 years and boy age 5 months).

JAMES ALFRED CANHAM, 5, Harvey's Row, Salcombe.
Ferryman, formerly Fisherman. Married. Age 46.
Wife, age 46.
Three Children (girl, age 17, epileptic ; boy, age 15 ; girl, age 4).
Mother, age 67, dependent for home, earns living as a nurse. Has two sons in
   Army, one age 27 and the other age 20.

ALBERT DISTIN, Croft Road, Salcombe.
Boatman. Married. Age 49.
Wife, age 36.
Three Children (boy age 5, girl age 4, girl age 13 months).

ALBERT EDWIN WOOD, 1, Victoria Place, Salcombe.
Boatbuilder. Single. Age 29.
No dependants.

SAMUEL MARCH DISTIN, 31, Buckley, Salcombe.
Fisherman. Married. Age 47.
Wife, age 46.
Daughter, age 21 ; one son, age 19, in Army ; and one son age 15, at Grammar
   School, Kingsbridge, where he obtained a Scholarship.

PETER HEATH FOALE, 7, Orestone, Salcombe.
Fisherman and Pilot. Married. Age 56.
Wife, age 55.
Daughter, age 22, suffers from Epilepsy.

JAMES HENRY COVE, 5, Robinson's Row, Salcombe.
Fisherman. Married. Age 36.
Wife, age 34.
Four Children (boy, age 10 ; girl 9 ; girl 8 ; and boy 2).

WILLIAM WAKEHAM LAMBLE, Russell's Court, Salcombe.
Age 47. Widower seven years.
Originally a Fisherman, then Garage Attendant, and recently Coastwatching.
One son, age 15, earning 8/- a week.
Mother (Widow, 20 years), age 69, and dependent on son for home.

WILLIAM J. FOALE, 7, Orestone, Salcombe.
Fisherman. Single. Age 32.
No dependants.

PETER HEATH FOALE, JUNR., 7, Orestone, Salcombe.
Fisherman. Single. Age 35.
No dependants.

THOMAS PUTT, 4, Church Street, Salcombe.
Fisherman. Married. Age 44.
Wife, age 43.
Three Children ; girl age 10 (step-daughter) ; girl age 2 ; and boy 1 week.
Stepson, in Navy, age 20.

WILLIAM FRANCIS CUDD, 26, Island Street, Salcombe.
Boatman. Married. Age 44.
Wife, age 37.
Two Children (boy age 4 ; girl age 16 months).

JOHN AMBROSE CUDD, 26, Island Street, Salcombe.
Rigger. Age 42. Single.
No dependants.

'Particulars of
Dependants of Men who
lost their Lives' published
by the Relief Fund Trustees
(RNLI)

Salcombe from Ilbertstow in the early 1900s. Bolt Head is in the background. *(Marshman's Postcards)*

their relief and that all of it should have been paid out to them. As it was, the limits placed on the allowances paid to the widows and children, meant that a surplus was indeed built up.* In 1957, this was absorbed into the RNLI's general investment fund, with the interest going towards the cost of maintaining the lifeboat.

The Lifeboat Fund Trustees, however, were acting strictly in accordance with guidance laid down by the Charity Commission at the time and this method of allocating disaster relief funds, with its fixed allowances, was to remain standard practice for many years to come. In 1966 relatives of the victims of the Aberfan Disaster were similarly aggrieved when it was proposed to use part of the relief fund to clear the coal tip that had devastated their village. And in 1982, following the terrible Penlee Lifeboat Disaster on 19 December 1981, it was only after a public outcry that all the money raised was paid to the relatives of those that died.

13   THE BOARD OF TRADE INQUIRY, JANUARY 1917

On 10 January 1917, an Inquiry into the loss of the *William and Emma* lifeboat was held in the Town Hall at Salcombe by Commander Warren Caborne, CB RD RNR, an Inspector to the Board of Trade.

Mr George Vaux conducted the proceedings on behalf of the Board of Trade and Lieutenant Keppel Foote RN represented the RNLI. Amongst the witnesses giving evidence were Felix Rubie, surveyor to the RNLI, the Coastguard Officer Leonard May, Samuel Distin's brother, James Distin, the previous coxswain, and the two survivors of the disaster, Eddie Distin and Bill Johnson. Dr William Cock, the Chairman of the local Lifeboat committee and Cyril Turner, the Honorary Secretary were also present.

* In 1969 this was valued at £4052, giving an annual yield of £207.

The Inspector in his report first described, in some detail, the *William and Emma*'s dimensions, form of construction and equipment. He then went on to examine evidence from her service and inspection records in order to confirm that she was safe and seaworthy. Inevitably the question arose as to whether a self-righting boat would have been a more appropriate choice for the station.

James Distin, who in 1903 had headed the deputation that had chosen the *William and Emma* in preference to a self-righter, gave evidence in support of that choice and the inquiry team subsequently visited the nearby Hope Cove station where the lifeboat *Alexandra*, another non self-righter of the Liverpool type, was a 'sister ship' of the *William and Emma*. They were 'much impressed with her roomy, solid, and seaworthy appearance'.

After hearing evidence from the eye witnesses about the nature of the disaster and the events which led up to it, the Inspector noted that 'notwithstanding the catastrophe that befell the *William and Emma*, the various witnesses expressed their unabated confidence in her'.

James Distin thought 'she was a real good seaworthy boat' and added that he had never heard anyone say anything against her. On the contrary, all the members of the crew had 'praised her up'. He also said that he had never seen worse weather at Salcombe, or a

The *William Cantrell Ashley*, a Liverpool type lifeboat at sea under full sail and with a full complement of 15 crew. On station at New Quay, Wales, from 1907 to 1948, she was the last of her type in service and, like the *William and Emma*, was a non self-righter. *(RNLI)*

worse sea on the Bar, than that experienced on 27 October, 1916. 'The weather was very, very rough. I have never seen so many seas on the Bar; you could count twelve seas in succession, one running after the other. In ordinary times you can only see from three to four seas.'

Eddie Distin said, as he had at the final inquest back in November, that he still had every confidence in the old boat, did not think they could get a better, and wished it were possible to have her back again. His views were endorsed by Bill Johnson. The Inspector recorded his findings as follows:

> The cause of the loss of the *William and Emma*, and thirteen of her crew, between 10am and 11am of the 27th of October last, was that, when returning to Salcombe after being called out for service and while changing from sails to oars preparatory to crossing the Bar, it then blowing a hard SW gale with a high sea, she was struck on the port quarter by a huge breaking wave which capsized her.
>
> The consensus of opinion was that any boat would have capsized when subjected to such a heavy breaking wave, but, however that may have been, and I am not disputing that view, I may point out that the *William and Emma* was caught at a great disadvantage, as her sails had just been lowered, her oars had not yet been brought into requisition, and she would be more or less out of command at the dangerous crisis. In saying this, I wish it to be distinctly understood that I do not desire to impute blame to anyone. All were, no doubt, doing their duty and their best, and even if there may have been a little over-confidence in the boat, one should not forget the old adage: '*De mortuis nil nisi bonum*'. ['Speak no ill of the dead'].
>
> In conclusion, I wish to record my deep sympathy with the relatives of those gallant men who risked and lost their lives in a brave attempt to render assistance to fellow creatures in peril on the sea.

View of the Bar in a storm looking east to Limebury Point in the foreground, with Gammon Head and Prawle Point beyond *(RNLI)*

Whilst fully recognising the bravery of the crew, the Inspector, in reaching his conclusions, clearly stopped short of endorsing its actions in attempting to re-cross the Bar. He raised doubts about the timeliness of the order to change from sail to oars and went on to say that 'there may have been a little over-confidence in the boat'. Yet, in his desire not to 'impute blame to anyone' or 'speak ill of the dead', he left his doubts hanging in the air. It is strange that these issues were not fully addressed in the inquiry.

Two questions remained unanswered. Firstly, should the sails have been lowered sooner? Rules governing the handling of pulling and sailing boats when attempting to land through heavy surf or broken water had been issued by the RNLI as far back as 1857. Coxswains were informed that 'as a general rule, when running for the land before a heavy sea, they will, invariably, if practicable, take in their sails before going into the broken water and take her to land under oars alone'. With a heavy breaker following the boat, the crew could hold water with their oars, or even back the boat towards it, in order to avoid broaching-to. However, a boat under sail, could not be backed or her way stopped with safety and so was in danger of being caught by a breaker and capsized.

Sam Distin did in fact order the sails to be lowered well before going into the broken water on the Bar. In fact, the boat was about half a mile* outside the Bar when he ordered 'Down main. Up after centre. Get out the drogue'.

AE Fairweather's contemporary photograph showing the position of the capsize marked with an 'X'. *(Fairweather Collection, Cookworthy Museum)*

---

* Eddie Distin said that the lifeboat 'must have been almost a mile from the Bar' when she capsized (see page 32). This would have placed her to seaward (i.e. south) of the Eelstone. However, the Inspector, in his report, stated that the lifeboat's position at the time was 'from one quarter to half a mile outside Salcombe Bar and near the Eelstone Rocks'. Both AE Fairweather's photograph above and Edward Chapman's painting on page 36 indicate that the *William and Emma* was to the north of the Eelstone when she was struck by the 'unlucky wave'.

It was when the crew were securing the halyards and before starting the very dangerous row in through the huge seas that were breaking right across the harbour entrance outside the Bar, that the boat was struck by the mountainous wave that capsized her.

The second question posed by the Inspector's conclusions is whether or not it was 'over-confidence in the boat' (and, presumably, in his crew as well) that led Sam Distin to state that 'She will go in; she is bound to go in, never fear...', when hindsight suggests that it might have been wiser to turn away and run downwind to a safer haven to the east?

The long haul round to Dartmouth, sailing wind against tide through very heavy seas, was clearly an uninviting prospect for a cold, wet and tired crew. In order to avoid the tidal races off the Prawle and Start Point headlands (particularly the latter which at near low water would be running at over two knots) it would have been necessary to stand well out to sea before entering Start Bay. Within the bay, heavy seas would have been breaking on the Skerries Bank. Avoiding these hazards would have meant a four or five hour passage to Dartmouth. There was nowhere closer to hand. Heavy surf would have prevented a landing on any of the beaches either side of Prawle Point i.e. Rickham and Moor Sands to the west and Horseley, Lannacombe and Great Mattiscombe to the east. Within Start Bay, the strong current running down between the coast and the Skerries would have ruled out making for the fishing villages at Hallsands, Beesands or Torcross.

Most of the crew were experienced fishermen or boatmen for whom crossing the Bar in varying states of wind and tide was a regular feature of their working lives. In addition to a sound working knowledge of local conditions, the men undoubtedly possessed superb seamanship skills and, as a result of long experience in handling the *William and Emma* in extreme conditions, total familiarity with her capabilities in heavy seas.

No one who was not in the boat had a better appreciation of the conditions that prevailed that day and no one came forward, after the event, with any evidence to suggest that the crew's brave decision to attempt the crossing was misjudged. The men were justifiably confident in their boat and could not have foreseen that they would be hit by a freak wave at the moment of maximum danger when they were changing from sail to oar. Today, one hundred years after the event, the only fair conclusion that can be reached is that it was sheer bad luck, in the shape of an 'unlucky wave', not over-confidence on the part of the coxswain and his crew, that led to the fatal capsize.

SALCOMBE LIFEBOAT. No. 250

14 THE REPLACEMENT LIFEBOAT

Although the town had been dealt a shattering blow, life had to go on. The country was still locked in a brutal war and, with the Germans stepping up their U-Boat campaign against British and allied merchant ships in Channel waters, there was an urgent need for a replacement lifeboat to rescue survivors. Within weeks of the disaster, a number of brave men volunteered to man a new boat, undeterred by the fate of the previous crew. Some had served on the old boat, but only one man, Eddie Distin, at just 26 years old, was judged to have the experience and qualities to take on the role of coxswain.

> *Eddie Distin:* It wasn't very long before it was decided that there ought to be another boat here. Well they came to me and asked me to take it [be coxswain], I said 'I don't really think I can'. Then they came down from London and they kept on pestering me until in the end I agreed. Then I had to

William and Emma's successor, the *Sarah Anne Holden* lifeboat, 1917-25 (Fairweather Collection. Cookworthy Museum)

go round and pick up some new blood and old. They were a rough crew at first, but we made out.

The new crew was in place when the Board of Trade Inquiry Inspector submitted his report at the end of January 1917, for in it he observed that:

It speaks well for Salcombe and its public spirit that, notwithstanding the great disaster which formed the subject of this Inquiry, a new lifeboat crew has already been formed in readiness for the time when they can be provided with a new craft.

The replacement lifeboat was sent down by rail from London to Kingsbridge on 22 April 1917. She was the *Sarah Anne Holden*, a 35ft x 8ft 6in (10.7m x 2.6m), ten-oared, self-righting boat. Built in 1900 by the Thames Iron Works, she had been stationed between 1900 and 1914 at Johnshaven, near Montrose on the Scottish North Sea coast. In March 1914 the *Sarah Anne Holden* had been badly damaged when the propeller of a fishing boat, which had been attempting to come alongside in stormy weather, tore a large hole in her planking. Subsequently withdrawn from service, the *Sarah Anne Holden* was sent down to Limehouse in London for repair and overhaul. During her fourteen years at Johnshaven, she saw service on 22 occasions and saved 15 lives.

The hospital ship *HMHS Asturias* aground off the Eelstone on 21 March 1917, not far from where the *William & Emma* capsized. *(Salcombe Maritime Museum)*

Another U-boat victim, the *SS Teesdale*, torpedoed three miles off Salcombe on 15 June 1917 *(wrecksite.eu)*

Upon her arrival at Kingsbridge, the *Sarah Anne Holden* was launched in the estuary and, with her new crew on board, was taken in tow by Lieutenant A E Wilcock in the port patrol boat – no doubt the same motor boat in which he had made the abortive rescue attempt after the *William and Emma* capsized.

It was unfortunate that the replacement lifeboat had not arrived in Salcombe a month earlier, for in the space of just three days (20-23 March 1917), four ships, the hospital ship *HMHS Asturias*, and the steamers *Hazelpark*, *Chorley* and *Maine*, were torpedoed just off Salcombe with the loss of 43 lives. However, two months after her arrival, she was able to go to the assistance of another U-Boat victim – the steamer *Teesdale*, bound from the Tyne for Gibraltar with coal, and with a crew of 26. Following reports of a large explosion at sea the lifeboat was launched at 10.10pm and some three miles offshore the crew found the *Teesdale*, sinking by the head after having been torpedoed. Several minesweepers were standing by the crippled vessel and the lifeboat brought three injured men ashore, before returning to assist in beaching the vessel.

For the next eight years the *Sarah Anne Holden* saw very little service and in 1925 the RNLI decided to close the station because of the difficulty of getting the lifeboat over the Bar and out to sea in south-easterly gales. This might be regarded as a vindication of the choice of the non self-righting *William and Emma*, which went to windward better than the self-righters. A further factor which led to the closure of the Salcombe station was that adequate protection to the South Devon coast was judged to have been provided by the new motor lifeboats at Torbay and Plymouth and by the re-opening in 1924 of the Hope Cove lifeboat station after a two-year closure.

However, in 1930 the Hope Cove station was again closed and Salcombe re-opened with its first motor lifeboat, the 40ft (12.2m) self-righting *Alfred and Clara Heath*, formerly stationed at Torbay. Eddie Distin was once again called upon to serve as coxswain and, in that capacity, carried out many notable rescues. On 13 December 1932, in a heavy swell, he succeeded in taking off 24 men who had scrambled onto the cliffs at Steeple Cove when their ship, the *SS Cantabria*, came ashore. When the famous Finnish windjammer, *the Herzogin Cecilie,* struck the Hamstone at Sewer (now Soar) Mill Cove in the early hours of 25 April 1936, Eddie and his crew managed to bring off 21 members of the crew and a lady passenger, in spite of the heavy swell.

Coxswain Eddie Distin, wearing his Silver and Bronze medals *(RNLI)*

In 1938, the *Alfred and Clara Heath* was replaced by a 46ft Watson motor lifeboat, the *Samuel and Marie Parkhouse*. In this lifeboat Eddie Distin continued to demonstrate outstanding leadership and bravery. For his superb seamanship in rescuing 62 men from the Belgian steamer *Louis Sheid,* which went ashore at Thurlestone on 7 December 1939, Eddie was awarded the RNLI's Silver Medal. Four years later he received the Bronze Medal for rescuing, in an easterly gale and heavy seas, eleven men from the Admiralty salvage craft *LC18*, in distress on The Skerries, in Start Bay on 4 December 1943.

Eddie Distin retired as coxswain in 1951 after nearly 30 years in the post, but the Distin family connection with the Salcombe lifeboat service – a connection which went back at least as far as 1886 when James Distin became coxswain – continues to this day. In 1962, shortly after the *Samuel and Marie Parkhouse* was replaced by the 47ft Watson class *Baltic Exchange,* Eddie's second son, Hubert 'Bubbles' Distin, became her coxswain. In 1972 'Bubbles' and his crew received the Thanks of the Institution Inscribed on Vellum for their bravery in saving five men from a Belgian trawler *Amelie Suzanne* which broke up and became a total wreck after going aground in Off Cove, near Bolt Head on 1 April 1972. Bubbles' son, Eric, also served as a crew member as did another of Eddie's grandsons, Brian Cooper. Brian's son, James, is a member of the current crew.

Coxswain H.W 'Bubbles' Distin *(RNLI)*

After 'Bubbles' died suddenly in December 1972, his father Eddie took the helm of the lifeboat which carried his ashes for scattering at sea. Ten months later, on the eve of the 57th anniversary of his survival from the 1916 disaster, Eddie himself died. Large numbers attended his funeral service at Salcombe Methodist Church on 4 November 1973. In the church which, appropriately, was decorated for the annual Harvest of the Sea, the Minister described Eddie Distin as 'one of the great stones of Salcombe on which this community has been built' and spoke of the loss of 'one of Salcombe's most illustrious sons'.

Today Eddie is still spoken of with great warmth and respect in Salcombe and, of the many objects on display in the town's Lifeboat Museum, the most cherished are his Silver and Bronze Medals, his Vellum Certificates and, above all, his watch – the pocket watch that stopped at 11.03am on the day of the disaster.

Eddie Distin's Silver and Bronze Medals and his pocket watch *(RNLI)*

Bill Johnson
(RNLI)

Eddie's fellow survivor, Bill Johnson, is said to have been so traumatised by the events of that terrible day that he never again ventured on water. He had spent all of his working life at sea – in the 1890s he had served as boatswain on the schooner *Little Pet* in the gruelling Newfoundland cod trade – and, on two occasions, before the lifeboat disaster, had narrowly escaped drowning. A 45 year old widower, with four children to support, he gave up his job as a waterman, and, after nearly nineteen years of service, his place in the lifeboat crew, to become a dealer in petrol and paraffin. He died in 1943 aged 71.

15   REMEMBERING THEIR SACRIFICE

On the town's war memorial, in Cliff Road, the names of the thirteen lifeboatmen who lost their lives in 1916 are to be found alongside those of the fallen of two world wars.* The memorial, a Celtic cross, stands in a beautiful and prominent location below Cliff House and it is fitting that their names are inscribed on the panel that directly overlooks the harbour.

The memorial was unveiled at a special ceremony on 7 April 1921 by Andrew McIlwraith, the local benefactor who played a major part in raising money for the Disaster Relief Fund. Taking pride of place at that ceremony were Coxswain Eddie Distin and his crew, all 'kitted out' in their kapok lifejackets.

An article in the 15 April 1921 edition of the *Kingsbridge Gazette*, referred to the 'happy inspiration' of including the names of the lost lifeboatmen on the memorial:

> It was proposed at the inauguration of the scheme that the memorial should be erected to the memory of the men who were killed in the War. By a happy inspiration there came a suggestion that it might include a memorial to the thirteen lifeboatmen who lost their lives in the terrible gale of October 1916, whilst returning from a wreck they had visited at the call of duty.
>
> What more fitting could there be than a joint memorial to heroes who died in the effort to save lives, as well to the heroes who made the supreme sacrifice in war to protect our homes and freedom from the oppressor.
>
> From the site of the Memorial can be seen the place where the disaster occurred. These men were also liable to be called for war duty, as they had to be prepared to go to the assistance of vessels in distress, when torpedoed by enemy submarines.
>
> The result of the decision meant that the trustees were empowered to contribute £100 to the Memorial – a worthy contribution.
>
> The inhabitants of Salcombe have just reason to be proud of the Memorial erected to her heroes, who gave their lives both in peace and in war, and will act as an inspiration to future generations.

* The names of the thirteen men are also inscribed on the RNLI Memorial at the RNLI Headquarters in Poole, Dorset

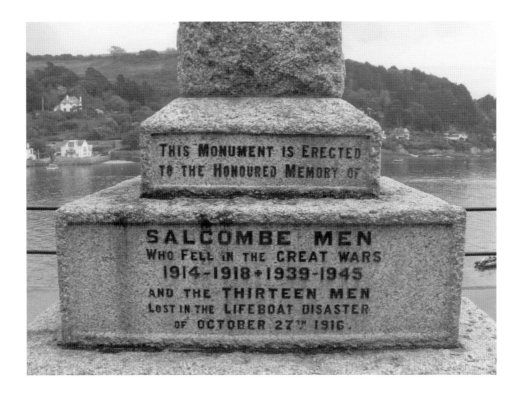

THIS MONUMENT IS ERECTED
TO THE HONOURED MEMORY OF

SALCOMBE MEN
WHO FELL IN THE GREAT WARS
1914-1918 + 1939-1945
AND THE THIRTEEN MEN
LOST IN THE LIFEBOAT DISASTER
OF OCTOBER 27TH 1916.

LIFEBOATMEN

CANHAM JAMES A.
COOK J. ASHLEY.
COVE JAMES H.
CUDD JOHN A.
CUDD FRANCIS W.
DISTIN ALBERT.

DISTIN SAMUEL M.
FOALE PETER H.
FOALE PETER H.
FOALE WILLIAM J.
LAMBLE WILLIAM W.
PUTT THOMAS.

WOOD ALBERT E.

Today, Salcombe is no longer the close-knit community it was a century ago. Yet, despite the changes wrought by time, there remains amongst local people a strong collective memory of the lifeboat disaster and of the impact it had on the town. Let us hope that the story of that fateful day continues to pass down through the generations, so that the selfless courage of the crew, and the tragic loss of all but two of their number, will always be remembered.

'Sacrifice supreme they offered,
Every soul save two,
Men who simply did their duty,
Yet were heroes true!'

The Salcombe War Memorial unveiling ceremony, April 7 1921.The lifeboat crew can be seen on the left. *(Fairweather Collection, Cookworthy Museum)*

Opposite page : The names of the thirteen men lost in the disaster inscribed on Salcombe War Memorial *(Author)*

(from 'The Bar' by R I Partridge)

THE CREW & THEIR FAMILIES

Sam Distin
(AE Fairweather)

SAMUEL DISTIN (Coxswain)

'Big Sam' Distin was a 47 year old fisherman at the time of the disaster. He had served as lifeboat cox since 1911, taking over from his elder brother James who had held the post for 25 years. The son of fisherman John Distin and Elizabeth March (both of whom had died before 1916), Sam had two other brothers, Albert, who also drowned in the disaster, and William (43). William was a regular member of the lifeboat crew but was unable to answer the call that day. All four brothers were born in Portlemouth.

In 1916 Sam was living with his wife Caroline (46) and two of his children, Verena (21) and Gerald (15), at 31, Buckley Street. Gerald was a pupil at Kingsbridge Grammar School. Another son, John (19), was a gunner in the Royal Garrison Artillery (he survived the First World War but died in 1941 whilst serving as a second lieutenant in the Royal Artillery). A non-smoker and an abstainer, Sam was said to have 'good earnings and a good home'. The cottage in Buckley Street had been bought from his mother-in-law and he owned a half share in a motor fishing boat and gear. Sam left Caroline £279 in his will.

ALBERT DISTIN

At 49, Albert Distin was two years older than his brother Sam. He was employed as a boatman and lived at Bigbury Cottages, Croft Road, Salcombe. His first wife was Eveline Putt. They married in 1895 but Eveline died in 1900 and their only child Daisy in 1914. In 1907 Albert married Annie Phillips from Crewkerne in Somerset. 1n 1916 Annie was 36 with three children, Albert aged 5, Madelin aged 4 and Gwendoline aged 13 months. Albert's wages were 26 shillings (£1.30) per week in the summer months and £1 a week in winter. He was insured with the Oddfellows Society for £10 at death. He had no other means and was only able to leave Annie £75 in his will.

Albert Distin
(AE Fairweather)

Peter Foale snr
(AE Fairweather)

PETER FOALE Senior (Second Coxswain)

The oldest member of the crew at 56, Peter Heath Foale senior was a fisherman and pilot. He was born in Salcombe in 1860, the son of Robert Foale, a former deputy coxswain of the Salcombe lifeboat. In 1889 Peter Foale piloted Lord Brassey's yacht *Sunbeam* across the Bar with Lord Tennyson aboard. In 1916 he lived with his wife Emily (55) and five children at 7, Orestone, Salcombe. Two of his sons, Peter Heath Foale junior (34) and William (31) were in the lifeboat crew and perished with him in the disaster. Their bodies were the first to be recovered and were buried on 1 November 1916. His other children were Cecil (29), Margaret (26) and Florence (22) who suffered from epilepsy.

Peter's average earnings during the war were about 15 shillings (75p) a week. He held the freehold of his cottage, which was worth about £8 a year and was insured in the Foresters against death for £12, in the Shipwrecked Mariners Society for £15 to £18, and the Pearl Insurance Office for £19. He owned three boats worth about £10 and left £190 in his will.

PETER FOALE Junior (Bowman)

Peter Heath Foale junior was 35, a fisherman, born in Salcombe. He was single with no dependants and lived with his parents at 7, Orestone, Salcombe and paid 10 shillings (50p) a week for his keep. He was insured in the Foresters for £12.

Peter Foale jnr
(AE Fairweather)

WILLIAM FOALE

Like his brother, William James Foale, age 32, was a fisherman, born in Salcombe. He too was single with no dependants and lived with his parents paying 10 shillings (50p) a week for board and lodging. He was insured in the Foresters for £12 and had about £70 in the Post Office savings bank.

JAMES CANHAM

James Alfred Canham was 46 when he died. He had been working as a ferryman on the Salcombe-East Portlemouth ferry and, prior to that, as a fisherman. Between 1904 and 1914 he had served as a naval reservist and his Royal Naval Reserve service record shows that he was only 5ft 5¾in (1.67m) in height. In 1910 he was awarded the RNR medal for Long Service and Good Conduct. During the Great War he served as a volunteer in the Salcombe Platoon, D Company, 2nd Battalion, Devon Volunteer Regiment and his funeral oration described him as 'a popular member of the Corps'. He also seems have been popular with his ferry passengers, one of whom described him after his death as 'poor Canham, the nice ferryman'. James' home in 1916 was 5, Harvey's Row, Salcombe where he lived with his wife Frances Ellen (46), and three of his five children, Emily (17), who had epilepsy, Ronald (15) and Doris (4). Sharing the home was James' mother-in-law, Mary Jane Gillard (67). James had two sons in the Army, Alfred Tolcher age 27 and Arthur age 20. Arthur served as a gunner in the 192 Siege Battery, the Royal Garrison Artillery and, ten months after her husband died in the lifeboat disaster, Frances suffered another tragic loss when Arthur was killed in action on the Western Front on 16 August 1917. James' wages as a ferryman had

William Foale
(AE Fairweather)

James Canham
(Andrea Helmsley)

been 25 shillings a week. He was insured in the Shipwrecked Mariners Society for £10-£12 and had boats worth about £8 but no savings. After his death his young son Ronald helped with the family finances by   working on the railway.

JAMES COVE

James Cove
(Diana Brown)

James Henry Cove was one of the two crew members whose body was never found. Born in Portlemouth, he was a 36 year old fisherman at the time of the disaster. James had married Beatrice Annie Stone (34) in 1905 and was father to Henry Elliot (10), Viola Rose (9), Beatrice Mary (8) and Cecil Arthur (2). The family lived at 5, Robinson's Row, Salcombe.

As a fisherman James earned between 10 and 15 shillings (50p-75p) a week in the winter but he was often laid up. This may have been due to poor health as he received 10 shillings a week from state insurance when he was ill. During the summer a gentleman named Mr Bird paid him 25 shillings (£1.25p) a week to be taken out fishing and 2s 6d (12½p) a week when he was not in Salcombe. He also worked at one time for a Colonel Cromie. The only items of property he left were two boats worth a few pounds.

ASHLEY COOK

Ashley Cook
(AE Fairweather)

At 24, John Ashley Cook, was the youngest member of the crew and one of the smallest in stature – he was 5ft 6in (1.67m) in height and weighed just over 9 stone (128 lbs/ 58kg). Like many of his peers, Ashley enlisted in the Devonshire Regiment soon after war was declared in August 1914, but in January 1915 he was discharged as medically unfit (by reason of 'painful flat feet preventing long marches'). On returning to Salcombe he married Edith Luscombe, a nurse from Loddiswell, and started to work again as a fisherman. He also helped his father, John Henry Cook, who ran a pleasure boat business at Council Quay. At his inquest Ashley's father said his son was not a recognised member of the lifeboat crew and he did not know he was volunteering that day. In fact he had sent for him to come and help him as one of his boats had broken adrift.

At the time of the disaster, Ashley and Edith had been renting a house at 49, Fore Street. Edith was 23 when her husband died and was left with two young sons, William aged 2 and Norman aged 5 months, to support. She must have struggled to cope as Ashley had a poor season in 1916. From his will she received effects worth £185, including a motor boat worth about £10. To add to her grief, Edith's two boys both died shortly after the loss of her husband. Norman died just five months after the disaster, in April 1917 and William in February 1918. Edith herself survived until she was 87.

FRANK CUDD

William Francis (Frank) Cudd was a 44 year old boatman, and a regular member of the lifeboat crew. Before the disaster Frank lived at 26, Island Street with his wife Florence (37), whom he had married in 1911, his son James Norman aged 4 and daughter Eva Mary aged 16 months. Other members of the household were his dependent father Ambrose Cudd aged 70 and his unmarried brother John (Jack) Ambrose Cudd (42) who also died in the disaster. Frank had been earning 25 shillings (£1.25p) a week as a boatman and Jack had paid 12 shillings (60p) a week for board and lodging. However, after they died Florence was left without any means of support, other than her father-in-law's old age pension and the money awarded by the relief fund. Strangely both Frank and his brother, Jack, had each lost an eye and for this reason both had been refused insurance and membership of a savings club.

Frank Cudd
(AE Fairweather)

JOHN CUDD

Frank's brother, John (Jack) Ambrose Cudd, was 42 when he died. He had lost an eye in the 1900 Chinese Boxer War whilst serving in the Royal Navy and, after spending some time in the merchant service, had settled down in Salcombe, as a rigger. He was a single man, living in his brother's house at 26, Island Street. He was a late volunteer for the crew, having only gone to watch the launch. Two of the crew were late so the cox shouted 'Who'll stand in then? What about it, Jack?' Jack replied 'I'm with you.'

John Cudd
(AE Fairweather)

WILLIAM LAMBLE

William Wakeham Lamble was a 47 year old widower when he died. He had been the last man to take his place in the lifeboat. Like a number of others in the crew, he was born in Portlemouth. Originally a fisherman, he later worked as a storekeeper in Plymouth and, prior to the disaster, as a part-time garage attendant in Salcombe, earning £1 a week. He also served with the Admiralty Coastguard as a Coast-watcher earning 21 shillings (£1.05p) a week. His wife Louisa had died in 1909 and so in 1916 he was living with his mother Mary Prowse Cook (69) and his son William, then aged 15, at 7, Russell Court, Salcombe. His daughter Kathleen was married with two children, Willie and Pat. He left no property and had not joined a savings club. His mother had been dependent on him for her home and she and her grandson had only the latter's income of eight shillings (40p) a week to live on. The Relief Fund accordingly granted her a widow's allowance of £1 1s (£1.05p). William's body was never found.

William Lamble
(AE Fairweather)

Thomas Putt
(AE Fairweather)

Thomas Putt
(Lin Morrissey)

Albert Wood
(AE Fairweather)

THOMAS PUTT

Thomas Putt was a 44 year old fisherman, born at Portlemouth. His wife Edith (42), whom he married in 1913, was the widow of James Friend, a coastguard, who had died in 1907. In 1916 Thomas and Edith lived at 4, Church Street, Salcombe with their children Gladys Mabel, aged 10 (Thomas' step-daughter) and Edith May aged 2. Their third child, Thomas Henry, was born the day after the disaster. There was also a stepson, James Friend, in the Navy. Thomas' average earnings were unknown but he had a small garden which he bought for £40 and savings of about £200 in the bank. He was insured in the Foresters for £12. As a widow, Edith received £1 1s (£1.05p) a week from the Disaster Fund and a maximum allowance of 9s (45p) for the three children until they reached 16. Nevertheless, in order to make ends meet, she still found it necessary to take in laundry and lodgers. In 1924, her widow's allowance was cut by half when she married Thomas' elder brother, William Henry (b1882).

For Edith, whose maiden name was Dignam, the loss of her husband in the lifeboat disaster was just one of many tragedies in her life – a life which was also to end in tragedy. Of her twelve brothers and sisters, five died young, including her brother William who drowned in Salcombe Harbour in 1885 aged 17. Her first husband, James Friend, died of disease in 1907 and their son, also James, died at Scapa Flow in 1918 whilst serving on *HMS Sunflower*. Edith and her third husband, William, were killed when a German bomb destroyed their home in Church Street, Salcombe on 8 September 1942. Her daughter-in-law, a newborn grandson and two step-grandsons aged 7 and aged 4 were also killed in the raid.

ALBERT WOOD

Albert 'Bert' Edwin Wood was a 29 year old boatbuilder and carpenter. The son of Edwin Wood, a Salcombe baker, he was single with no dependants, earned 28 shillings (£1.40p) a week, and paid 10 shillings (50p) a week board and lodging to his parents with whom he lived at 1, Victoria Place. He had three boats worth approximately £25. Amongst those mourning his loss was his fiancée, Daisy.

The Survivors

EDWIN DISTIN

Eddie Distin was born in Warsash on the River Hamble in Hampshire in 1891. His father, William James Distin, a fisherman, had been born in Salcombe in 1868 but moved to Warsash after his marriage to a local girl, Julia Pounsett (1868-1948). William is believed to have been lost at sea in the fishing vessel *Gem* in 1895 when Eddie was just four years old. His grandparents in Salcombe, William and Emma Distin, took him into their care and, in 1911, Eddie, an unmarried fisherman, was living with them at 2, Orestone, Salcombe. William and Emma died in 1914 and 1913 respectively. Perhaps they were 'watching over' him when the lifeboat, which bore their names, capsized in 1916.

Eddie married Gertrude Youlden (1892-1958) in 1914. In 1916, at the time of the disaster, he was 25 years old. Eddie was one of the first to volunteer when the RNLI recruited a new lifeboat crew in 1917 and served as coxswain of the replacement lifeboat, the *Sarah Anne Holden* between 1917 and 1925. From 1925 to 1929 there was a break in service when the lifeboat station was closed.

Between 1930-8 Eddie was cox of the *Alfred and Clara Heath* and between 1938 and his retirement in 1951, cox of the *Samuel and Marie Parkhouse*. He was awarded the Institution's Silver Medal for the rescue of 62 men from the Belgian vessel, the *Louis Sheid,* which broke up and sank off the coast near Thurlestone on 7 December 1939. He was also awarded the Bronze Medal of the Institution after the rescue of eleven men from an Admiralty salvage craft which went down in Start Bay on 4 December 1943. Eddie retired in 1951 after nearly thirty years' service as coxswain. His second son, Hubert (Bubbles) Distin (1919-1972), was appointed coxswain in 1962. Eddie died in October 1973 aged 82. (Bubbles had died suddenly of bronchitis in December 1972).

Coxswain Eddie Distin *(RNLI)*

Eddie in retirement *(RNLI)*

WILLIAM JOHNSON

Bill Johnson was a waterman aged 45 in 1916, having been born in Salcombe about 1871. In 1911 he was a widower, living with his four children at 1, Buckley St., Salcombe. In 1916, his son William was aged 17, and his daughters were Kathleen (14), Sylvia (12) and Marion (6). After the disaster Bill lived at the Wigwam, Raleigh Road, Salcombe and became a petrol dealer. Known locally as the 'Oil Baron' or 'Oil King' he had a depot on Brewers Quay, Island Street and owned a number of properties in the town. He died in 1943 aged 71.

Bill Johnson *(AE Fairweather)*

Crossing the Bar

Sunset and evening star,
And one clear call for me!
And may there be no moaning of the bar,
When I put out to sea,

But such a tide as moving seems asleep,
Too full for sound and foam,
When that which drew from out the boundless deep
Turns again home.

Twilight and evening bell,
And after that the dark!
And may there be no sadness of farewell,
When I embark;

For tho' from out our bourne of Time and Place
The flood may bear me far,
I hope to see my Pilot face to face
When I have crost the bar.

Alfred, Lord Tennyson

Sources

Primary Sources
Contemporary newspaper reports in the *Salcombe Times, Kingsbridge Gazette* and *Western Morning News*
Lifeboat Journal, February 1st 1917, RNLI
Salcombe Lifeboat Disaster, The Devonian Year Book 1917
Report of the Inquiry into the Wreck of the William and Emma on October 27th 1916, issued by the Board Of Trade on March 9th 1917
Disaster Relief Fund. Deed of Trust papers prepared by C.E. Turner, Solicitor, Salcombe (and Honorary Secretary of the Local Lifeboat Committee) for the RNLI
Undated transcript of an interview with Eddie Distin by a member of the Salcombe Museum Society
Miscellaneous papers in the RNLI's Archive at Poole

Secondary Sources
Lifeboat Journal, September 1966. Article entitled *'Focus on Salcombe'* by Christopher Elliott, RNLI
The Salcombe Lifeboat Disaster by James Fairweather Tall. A series of articles published in the 'Three-in-One' Parish Magazine, 2006

Acknowledgements

My sincere thanks to all those who helped in some way with the completion of this book. I am particularly indebted to Simon Evans, the Lifeboat Operations Manager at Salcombe RNLI and Andrew Arthur, Launching Authority, Treasurer & Training Co-ordinator, for their encouragement and support and to the following for their help and advice: Malcolm Darch, world-renowned model-making ship-wright/yachtbuilder, maritime historian and author of '*Salcombe and Hope Cove Lifeboat History*' published in 1984; Edward Hannaford, Salcombe lifeboatman from 1951 to 1981 and second coxswain/mechanic 1973-1981; Frank Smith MBE, Salcombe lifeboat coxswain 1988-2001; Andy Thomson, RYA Yachtmaster Ocean Instructor and my successor as Station Manager at NCI Prawle Point, and Carol Waterkeyn, Editor/Review Editor at RNLI Headquarters.

I am also extremely grateful to Jenny Brown and Theresa Thomson for proof reading the manuscript; Holly Trubshawe, Curator of Kingsbridge Cookworthy Museum, for help with photographs; Jeremy and Amanda Linn for taking me out on their boat to view relevant locations from the sea; the marine artist Paul Deacon for allowing me to reproduce his superb painting on the front cover and to alter it by erasing the mizzen sail; Hilary 'H' Ashford of Salcombe History Society for providing me with newspaper transcripts; Ken Prowse, Chairman of Salcombe History Society and my colleagues at Salcombe Maritime Museum for their support and also to Lin Morrissey for help in researching the crew and their descendants.

A number of descendants – all granddaughters – kindly provided much useful information: Marilyn Ayre (Bill Johnson), Carol Baxendale (Eddie Distin), Diana Brown (James Cove), Andrea Helmsley (James Canham), Lin Morrissey (Thomas Putt), Jill Pridham (Albert Distin) and also Caroline Utin, granddaughter-in-law of Bill Johnson. Margaret Harrison, granddaughter of James Distin, the lifeboat cox between 1885-1911, also provided valuable information about the Distin family.

Further Information and Places To Visit

Salcombe Lifeboat Museum, Union Street, Salcombe, TQ8 8BZ.
Tel: 01548 842158
Website: www.salcombelifeboat.co.uk
Opening times: March-October, daily.
Included in the displays are Eddie Distin's watch, which stopped shortly after the lifeboat capsized, a superb collection of lifeboat models by Malcolm Darch including the *William and Emma,* and much interesting information about Salcombe's 'pulling and sailing' lifeboats and their crews.

Salcombe Maritime Museum, The Old Council Hall, Market Street, Salcombe, TQ8 8DE, (below the Tourist Information Centre).
Tel: 01548 843080 (opening hours only).
Website: www.salcombemuseum.org.uk
Opening times: April-October, daily.
'A Treasure Trove of Salcombe's Maritime Past' with a magnificent collection of ship models, paintings, shipwreck and WWI & 2 artefacts, as well as many other exhibits from Salcombe's heyday as a schooner port. The display in the Wreck Room tells the story of the disaster and includes a fine model of the *William and Emma,* as well as a section of her hull planking and one of her oars.

National Coastwatch Prawle Point Visitor Centre, Prawle Point, East Prawle. Tel: 01548 511259 (opening hours only)
Website: www.nci-prawlepoint.org.uk
Opening times: 9-5 daily plus evenings in the summer.
The Visitor Centre and Lookout are worth visiting to see the work of the modern-day successors to Chief Officer May's team of coast-guards and also for the panoramic view from Prawle Point of the route taken by the crew of the *William and Emma.*

National Trust Overbecks, Sharpitor, Salcombe, TQ8 8LW.
Tel: 01548 842893
Website: www.nationaltrust.org.uk/overbecks/
Opening times: see website.
In 1916, nurses and convalescing soldiers from the former Sharpitor
VA Hospital played their part in the attempted rescue of the lifeboat
crew. Today, Overbecks is worth visiting for the beauty of its gardens
and setting, its fascinating collections in the house and for the splen-
did views it offers of the coast between the Bar and Prawle Point.

South Devon AONB and the SW Coast Path
The magnificent coastal scenery between Prawle Point and Bolt Head,
the scene of the disaster, is best explored by walking the SW Coast
Path. Walking guides can be downloaded from:
www.southdevonaonb.org.uk/explore/walks-trails/

2016 Centenary Commemorations.
To mark the centenary of the disaster, Salcombe RNLI, in association
with the National Trust, are proposing to erect two memorial stones
overlooking the scene of the fatal capsize – one near Limebury Point
and the other on the Bolt Head side of the estuary above the
Eelstone. A full programme of commemorative events will take place
in Salcombe on October 27th 2016.

'Answering the Call.'
The Salcombe
lifeboats below
Prawle Point
(Chris Tizzard)